CARING FOR UNEMPLOYED PEOPLE

A Study of the Impact of Unemployment on Demand for Personal Social Services

Prepared for the Association of Metropolitan Authorities
by
Susan Balloch,
Chris Hume,
Brian Jones
and
Peter Westland

Published for the
Association of Metropolitan Authorities
by
BEDFORD SQUARE PRESS | NCVO

Published by
BEDFORD SQUARE PRESS of the
National Council for Voluntary Organisations
26 Bedford Square
London WC1B 3HU

ISBN 0 7199 1151 6

First published 1985

Typeset by Electronic Village, Richmond, Surrey

Printed and bound in England by
Biddles of Guildford, Surrey

CONTENTS

Preface

This study was carried out to substantiate the volume of anecdotal evidence already accumulated by local authorities about the impact of rapidly increasing unemployment on the demand for social services. Our overriding concern was that the final report should be objective and that its conclusions 'speak for themselves'.

We were fortunate to secure the services of Susan Balloch, an academic researcher, who not only brought a wealth of valuable experience but also a fresh view to some of the problems which beset the personal social services. To ensure the independence and integrity of its conclusions the research was guided by an independent steering group, consisting of Directors of Social Services and academics.

The findings of the report are unequivocal; a report which discusses how local authorities are struggling to meet demands which threaten to overwhelm some key services; a report which highlights the decline in the availability of services in the face of increasing need in the growing numbers of people who seek them.

The report raises many questions which point to the need for further investigation, for more sensitivity to unemployment as an issue affecting service delivery within social services departments, and for even greater efforts towards improving the co-operation between different agents of social welfare policies including housing, education and social security. It challenges local authorities in general and social services departments in particular to review their responses to the need for services relevant to unemployed people.

My personal view is that, if this report reflects the true nature of the impact of unemployment on social services nationally then a major crisis is imminent. The personal social services seem to be moving from a situation of being providers of barely adequate services for the poor towards becoming underfunded, overstretched and in some cases overwhelmed services for the oppressed. When the majority of persons referred to the social services are unwaged, when they are becoming poorer, when their chance of decent housing is declining and where their access to jobs is much less, then it is no exaggeration to describe many users of social services as an oppressed class. Local government must meet this challenge. Its services must be improved and extended to allow an individual the right to participate in activities which increase rather than diminish self esteem, which make unemployed people feel valued rather than forgotten and to combat the incidence of health, financial and social problems which often accompany unemployment.

This is a report which must be taken seriously by individual local authorities, by local authority associations and by central government. The Association is grateful not only to the research team and social services secretariat but also to the authorities which gave so generously of their time and facilities.

Tessa Jowell
Chair of Social Services Committee
Association of Metropolitan Authorities

Acknowledgements

Many people have given help and support to this project. In particular we should like to thank David Blunkett, Tessa Jowell and the AMA Social Services Committee members who first proposed the idea, the late Fred Lunn, former Leader of Barnsley MDC whose timely intervention secured funding from the Association, Claudine McCreadie whose preliminary pilot study convinced us that the project was both necessary and vital, and Professor Adrian Webb for his advice and inspiration.

The Steering Committee, led by David Plank, Director of Social Services, Hounslow helped us to identify and maintain a sense of direction, encouraged us when progress was difficult to discern, gave robust and constructive criticism of our drafts and maintained throughout a confidence at times greater than our own. Many researchers and commentators gave freely of their time interpreting their publications and their current work in related fields; the GLC library gave assistance in our search for and review of literature; the GLC Research and Intelligence Division at some sacrifice of its own priorities processed all of our referrals data having first helped us adapt our questionnaire for computer analysis. Without this help Chapter 7 would not have been possible in its current form.

Finally, our thanks must go to the Directors of Social Services, Researchers, Managers and Social Workers of our sample authorities, for their patience, tolerance, creative thinking, time and enthusiasm without any of which the project simply could not have been launched or completed. A special mention should be made of Coventry Social Services Department which both acted as our pilot authority and further participated in the actual survey as a representative of the West Midlands area. Thanks also to Lorraine Coles our Secretary, Jean Dawes and her word processing team whose skills eased us through many revisions and to Julian Hodgson of the Bedford Square Press for many helpful suggestions and his eagle eye for grammatical infelicities.

Responsibility for the outcome is, of course, entirely ours.

Susan Balloch Chris Hume
Brian Jones Peter Westland

June 1985

Introduction

1. In a few short years, since the later 1970s, mass unemployment has become a way of life for well over 1 in 10 of the population. To most people unemployment is viewed as an economic statistic. There is now growing evidence that unemployment creates social problems. Links with increased suicide, mental illness and marital breakdown have recently been reported. As the personal social services deal with these and other social problems, what impact has unemployment had on social services clients? Furthermore what has been our response to any change in needs?

2. AMA authorities contain some of the worst unemployment black spots in England. These areas already manifested severe social problems requiring social services intervention prior to the current recession. Has unemployment exacerbated these problems? These were the questions this inquiry sought to answer.

3. In a written answer to a question in the House of Commons in February 1984 the Secretary of State for Social Services stated that local authority budgets for 1983-84 'showed aggregate spending on personal social services at about 12% in volume terms above the level five years ago in 1978-79'. There were, of course, it was added, no targets for local authority expenditure on the personal social services and authorities were free to determine their own priorities in this context.[1] What did not gain mention was the considerably different economic situation in which the personal social services have to operate in the 1980s, one in which a 'free' choice of priorities is made difficult by the constant pressure of high unemployment. This pressure has now been officially acknowledged, both by the Secretary of State for Social Services at the Joint Social Services Conference in September 1984 and by the Chancellor of the Exchequer. When this AMA research was first considered however, the human problems arising from the continuation of high unemployment and the consequently intensified demands for help from the social services had received scant public attention.

4. As the current recession intensified Chairs and Directors of Social Services in metropolitan areas began to express concern that growing unemployment may be leading to increased demand on their social services resources. This culminated in the AMA Social Services Committee resolving that an attempt should be made to identify whether there was any evidence to corroborate the widespread feeling of both officers and members in local government that unemployment was causing increased demand. This therefore resulted in the AMA conducting a survey within member authorities.

5. The task of this research study, initially, was to collect as much hard data as possible to demonstrate the extent and nature of the social services needs resulting from growing unemployment. This objective was achieved although there is scope for the collection of further information. Data was collected from a sample of eight AMA authorities — representing nearly 12% of all AMA social services authorities with a total resident population of 2,300,000 people. Of this total population approximately 236,000 people, or 17.35% of the adult population were unemployed.

This report begins, in Chapter 1, by exploring the nature and size of the unemployment problem and the social consequences for specific groups in society. The report then progresses to describe how the problem of researching the impact of unemployment on social services demand was tackled; including the selection of a sample of local authorities for detailed study.

In Chapter 2 the report explores whether employment opportunities for physically and mentally handicapped people have declined, what this means for demand on places at day centres and sheltered workshops and on our ability to rehabilitate handicapped people.

Chapter 3 examines the consequences of the increased presence of young people in community homes during the working day and the impact of unemployment on the ability of young people to leave care successfully.

Chapter 4 asks whether unemployment is a cause of mental illness and consequently reduces the ability to rehabilitate mentally ill clients.

In Chapter 5 the report looks at the financial impact of unemployment and the possibility that this leads to more people seeking advice and help from social services departments.

Chapter 6 is a brief examination of the argument that youth unemployment is closely linked with increased juvenile crime and of the responses of intermediate treatment officers and programmes to this contention. The survey also attempted to collect data on unemployment and child abuse, but research into this important subject proved inconclusive. A summary of the limited findings can be found in Appendix D.

Many of these individual themes, and some others, also emerge from a survey of social work referrals within each of the sample authorities. Some of the results of this survey are summarised in Chapter 7.

Whatever emerges from this survey is largely tentative and exploratory. The subject was previously largely unresearched. This study is the first stage in developing evidence of a link between unemployment and social services demand. Some clear trends are identified; in other instances insufficient evidence is available but common-sense assumptions are reinforced and the subject clearly merits further research. Some of the most convincing findings and suggestions for further work are set out in the final chapter.

Chapter 1
Unemployment: Researching the Social and Economic Context

Unemployment: Its Extent and Nature

1. In the context of the post-war period, mass long-term unemployment is a recent phenomenon. Until the mid-1960s unemployment in the UK rested at rather less than 2% of the population. Some areas such as the North East and Northern Ireland had higher levels of unemployment during this period than other parts of the country, due to a 'structural' unemployment reflecting the decline of traditional industries. Even in these areas however the numbers out of work for more than six months were low. The majority of unemployment could be described as 'frictional', i.e. the result of those job changes generally regarded as a normal part of a healthy economy. This 2% showed a slow increase to 4% in the early 1970s. The present recession brought with it a far more serious state of affairs. From July 1979, when unemployment was officially recorded at 1.39 million, or 5.9% of the population, the numbers of unemployed rose dramatically to reach 3.19 million, or 13.4% of the population, by July 1982.[1]

2. Official statistics have suggested smaller increases in this figure over the last two years, with numbers in February of this year recorded as 3,323,676 or 13.7% of the work force. Critics of unemployment statistics challenge official figures as deceptively low estimates and argue that a more accurate estimate of the unemployed today would already be over four million.[2]

3. In October 1982 a change in the method of collecting unemployment statistics — from recording by registered unemployed to recording only those drawing benefit — resulted in underestimation of the real unemployment problem. This change particularly affected the numbers of women shown as unemployed as they are often treated as dependent on a partner's income and so cannot receive benefit. Similarly men over 60 now no longer need to register for social security credits. Even before this change, however, the figures took account of those who did not register as unemployed. Bradford Metropolitan District has estimated that if all the unregistered unemployed people actually seeking work were added to official figures, locally the number of jobless women would increase by 42% and men by 7%.[3]

4. Since the mid-1970s those areas of former prosperity and full unemployment have suffered as much as those areas with longer standing structural unemployment. The West Midlands, for example, experienced a rise in the unemployment rate from 1.8% in 1973, to 5.6% in 1979, to 9.4% in 1980,[4] and this is an area where full employment had previously been the norm. The devastating effects of this on Coventry, for example, have been graphically outlined by Hill and by Taylor.[5,6]

5. Whilst regional variations have tended to diminish as unemployment has risen, differences still exist between various parts of the country and show up particularly in the long-term unemployment rates of areas such as the North and North West.[7] Furthermore there is an uneven spread of unemployment within any region or local authority area, a factor which unemployment figures generally do not indicate. Inner-city areas are almost always harder hit than their outer suburbs and pockets of high unemployment are to be found even in areas of the affluent South East. An exception has to be made, however, for the outlying estates of long established cities that were built in the 1950s and 60s. Recent evidence suggests that such areas are now even more impoverished and deprived than the inner-city areas from which their populations originally came.[8]

The Impact of Unemployment on Certain Groups

6. The geographical distribution of unemployment makes little sense, however, without a further appreciation of its social distribution. Unemployment has always particularly affected the semi-skilled and unskilled workers of social classes IV and V — and this is still the case — but even within these classes certain groups are particularly vulnerable. In particular the following groups are most severely affected.

7. (i) Ethnic Groups Studies by Daniel and Smith in the late 1960s indicated the extent to which ethnic minority groups were more vulnerable to unemployment than whites and had more trouble finding jobs. With the growth of unemployment, the situation worsened, as revealed by Smith's national survey in 1976.[9] More recently a third Policy Studies Institute report has been published with evidence on the key differences between black and white employment patterns and the changes that have taken place as unemployment has risen since the mid 70s.[10] The unemployment rates among black men and women are found to be much higher than for the white population, partly this is due to the lower average age of black than of white men and women meaning that a greater proportion are economically active. For West Indian men and Asian women the proportions of registered unemployed were found to be twice as high as for whites; for Asian men and West Indian women, one and a half times as high as for whites. Changes in the unemployment rate between 1974 and 1982 were also found to have affected black people to a greater extent than white.

8. Similarly, a study of the young unemployed in the West Midlands found that 23% of young people registered in Birmingham careers offices in November 1981 were of ethnic minority origin.[11] A recently published social survey of Bradford has underlined the plight of young Asians, as well as of the ethnic minority in general,[12] and a CRE document has expressed grave concern at the depressing employment prospects of school leavers.[13]

9. (ii) Women Workers Two aspects distinguish women's work in the 1980s — first, it is heavily concentrated in particular industries such as clothing and footwear manufacture and services; and second, it is characterised by part-time, low-paid employment. The growth of the service sector and the shortening of the working week, with the growth of more flexible working patterns, might reasonably be supposed to have improved women's employment prospects, but since the mid-70s this has not been the case. Women's unemployment rose much faster than that of men in the 1970s, increasing sevenfold in comparison with a doubling of the rate among men.[14] Yet these official figures were and still are, an underestimate. The 1979 General Household Survey found that half of all married women and a quarter of those unmarried, who declared themselves unemployed, were not registered. Given the recognised contribution of women's earnings to family budgets, such unregistered unemployment is a cause for great concern.[15] Female unemployment seems especially likely in those poorer families where a second income would make the difference between a bearable standard of living and poverty. For a variety of reasons, too, women are more likely to be unemployed where their husbands are unemployed.[16] In fact 'family unemployment' is fast becoming an easily recognisable phenomenon.[17] Within the female workforce young women and women 'returners' seem especially at risk from unemployment. Women under 25 have the highest unemployment rate of any group in the country and women returners, who generally go back into employment at a lower level and status than that at which they left to raise their families, clearly have fewer opportunities now than in the 1960s and 1970s.

10. (iii) Youth Unemployment Young people, a group described as 'having the most time and energy to bear the rest of Britain a grudge',[18] have also become a significant and perhaps most worrying feature of the unemployment scene. In Britain, where 1,750,000 young people under 25 are officially unemployed, 350,000 have been unemployed for a year or longer.[19] A recent study of a Birmingham suburb recorded an increase of 280% in youth unemployment in the West Midlands between January 1979 and June 1982, a figure which rose to 400% in the actual survey area of 'Castlehill'. In this context the increase was related firstly to decline in skilled and semi-skilled employment in car manufacturing and secondly to the growing number of school leavers in an area with an unbalanced age distribution.[20] This situation is in no way peculiar to the Midlands. Knowsley in the North West has the highest youth unemployment level in Britain with an unenviable record 85% of school leavers unemployed or serving on YTS.[21] Not only do these youngsters lack a wage; they also lack the chance to assume an adult role and acquire an adult identity, a possibility that becomes increasingly remote the longer the spell of unemployment continues.

11. Nearly half of all 16-year-old school leavers now proceed to YTS. Recent evidence from the MSC has suggested an improving situation with nearly 70% of those leaving YTS going on to jobs or further education. Youthaid has however described this as a seriously misleading statement, given that the MSC's evidence was drawn from three surveys looking at only 2% of all trainees, over half of whom had not responded. Youthaid's own analysis suggests only about half of YTS trainees go into jobs and an unknown figure actually abandon their scheme before it is completed. Where young school leavers do find work, it appears that they go into manufacturing and production rather than into the service industries where employment prospects are better.

12. (iv) Older Workers Older workers are very seriously affected by unemployment also. In 1921 approximately 80% of men worked into their late 60s. Today that figure has fallen to 10%.[22] Older workers have become less and less common in employment and have fallen victim to the belief that younger workers, in times of high unemployment, deserve priority in getting jobs. Although some may be happy to retire early, for many others early retirement or redundancy simply means an early entry into poverty. For the out-of-work 50-year-old the chances of obtaining another job are now very limited. A 1977 study of job vacancies at MSC employment offices found 27.5% were explicitly disqualified by an upper age limit and a similar PEP study found only a quarter of vacancies open to those of over 50.[23]

13. The financial, social and health implications of unemployment for older workers are far-reaching. Parker's survey in 1980 found many of the early retired in financial difficulties, with few having adequate occupational pensions.[24] Evidence points to deterioration in social well-being and physical health although research in this particular field is lacking.

14. (v) The Long-term Unemployed The number of unemployed recorded at any one time is the net product of flows into and out of unemployment. In the past the length of time spent unemployed by individuals has on average been short, but in the last four years long-term unemployment, of over one year's duration, has become much more extensive, as indicated by a fall in the relative numbers of people moving out of the unemployment register. It is estimated that the numbers of long-term unemployed have risen from about 300,000 in 1980 to over one million today. In January 1985, those unemployed for over one year numbered 1,316,000 of whom 365,000 were aged under 25.[25] The long-term unemployed are a fundamentally impoverished group.

15. A recent DHSS cohort study looking at the characteristics of 2,300 men sampled in 1978 from new unemployment registrations found that the previous earnings of the newly unemployed were well below the national average. Fifty per cent had had earnings in the bottom fifth of the earning distribution, only a third of wives were working compared with over a half for the population as a whole and many had recent experiences of unemployment, half in the previous year and three quarters in the previous five years. The poverty of this sample indicated the lack of resources suffered by many of the unemployed for whom the opportunity to save or invest has been lacking.[26]

16. These findings have been more recently confirmed by Bradshaw's inquiry into the living standards of the long-term unemployed. He found that the unemployed as a whole were poorer than even very low wage earners. The long-term unemployed were living on just over half of the gross income of the long-term employed and had only just over two-thirds of their mean disposable income. The longer they remained unemployed, the lower became their expectations and the higher their proportionate expenditure on the bare necessities of life.([27])

17. (vi) Other Groups In addition to the above, other groups disproportionately affected by unemployment include: physically handicapped people, mentally handicapped people and mentally ill people. These groups are vulnerable in better economic times having poorer educational, physical and social skills. In times of high unemployment, when employers have a large pool of potential employees or applicants, they tend to employ the most qualified and able.[28] Similarly when redundancies are necessary employers tend to release handicapped and mentally ill people first. The employment problems of these groups are discussed in more detail later in the text in view of their reliance on social services in both good and bad economic times.

The Social Effects of Unemployment

18. Although there is some limited published research on the social impact of unemployment there have as yet been no national investigations specifically on unemployment and social services needs. Some recent studies have identified direct links between lack of employment and specific social problems. For example unemployment and mental illness;[29] unemployment and suicide;[30] and unemployment and crime.[31] Much of this research has not been related to demand on social services departments, although clearly many of the identified social impacts relate to social services clients or potential clients. There is clearly an identifiable need for original research on the effect of unemployment on social services departments' workloads.

Researching the Impact of Unemployment on Demand for Personal Social Services

19. The Association first began to explore this subject following growing concern expressed by member authorities about the lack of recognition both locally and nationally of the precise impact of unemployment on social services budgets and workloads. Exploratory work reviewed literature and research and concluded that in order to establish a factual relationship between unemployment and social services demand, firsthand data would have to be collected. To this end the Association sent a questionnaire to all social services authorities in membership of the AMA to ascertain whether the kind of data available might illuminate the relationship. This survey revealed a lack of data on employment status of social services clients. Consequently the Association's Policy Committee agreed to finance a research project which aimed to collect data indicating the impact of unemployment on social services demand. The findings from the earlier work were incorporated into a research plan for a 12-18 month study. A Steering Group was convened in October 1983 comprising five Directors of Social Services and two Academics to direct the project. A list of members of the steering group is to be found in Appendix A.

20. We attempted to measure the impact of unemployment on demand for social services only. We did not examine the latent or unmet need and attendant social problems resulting from unemployment which clearly exist but for which social services do not provide help. Demand in this context refers to 'expressed need'[32] i.e. those people in need presenting themselves to departments for help or actually being helped.

21. To identify further some of the attendant social problems and their effects on the personal social services, particular types of services were singled out for examination. Of the five service areas chosen, the first, dealing with sheltered workshops, day centres and sheltered industrial groups (SIGs), would throw some light on the added difficulties increased unemployment might create for the handicapped; the second, considering juvenile crime rates and IT schemes, would show whether there were increasing strains on the services as a result of unemployment and delinquency — this also included some work on child abuse; the third, dealing with children in care and their employment prospects, might throw some light on the additional difficulties those who have been in care have in coping with an adult environment due to increased unemployment; the fourth, looking at mental health referrals and the fifth, looking at financial referrals, were intended to examine further the links between these and unemployment and show whether additional strains were being placed on services.

22. These five were selected because not only did they appear from previous work to be the most likely to produce relevant information, but also because they were sufficiently self-contained to permit some profitable research within the time available.

23. The lack of direct numerical data on the employment status of clients meant there was no possibility of mounting a study to test direct causal links between unemployment and social services demand. Instead an approach was developed which involved compiling a body of evidence, both quantative and qualitative, which might indicate the existence of a relationship. In some of the five service areas this might be indicated more directly than in others.

Material collected would not be comparable between authorities' therefore any attempts at statistical correlation would also be inappropriate.

24. Backing this up, a month-long referrals survey was designed to show whether or not new clients of the social services had a background of unemployment and exhibited problems directly related to this.

The Sample

25. To maximise the use of resources the strength of the relationship between unemployment and social services demand in these five service areas was examined in a sample of authorities. The need to strike a balance between the credibility of results and resources available led to the selection of a sample comprising eight authorities.

26. This sample was not selected randomly. This was considered unnecessary as the study did not involve testing a causal hypothesis and direct comparisons between authorities were not possible due to the variation in data and definitions from one area to another. The only constraint was the decision to restrict the sample to members of the AMA in view of our special relationship and role. Given these basic premises the aim was to establish a sample balancing the following criteria: (i) Geographical Distribution; (ii) Type of Authority; (iii) Socio-Economic Structure; (iv) Unemployment Level; (v) Political Control; (vi) Population; and (vii) Service Levels. These criteria are described in more detail in Appendix B.

27. It was also decided that as well as including authorities identified by the criteria above, it would also be of advantage to include an authority with a much lower level of unemployment. There are several advantages in this: firstly, the increase in the national level of unemployment may affect more prosperous areas as well as the inner city and larger estates; secondly, there may be pockets of unemployment even in prosperous areas causing hardship; and thirdly it would establish a marker against which to consider the severity of problems in other areas.

28. Using readily available data and applying the above criteria the following sample was selected:-

Table 1 — The Sample

	Population (1981 census)	Unemployment (January 1985) No.	Rate
Tower Hamlets	144,000	12,215	21.8%
Lambeth	245,000	25,507	19.4%
Harrow	199,400	6,254	6.4%
Walsall	265,300	—	—
Manchester	457,500	44,764	23.6%
Knowsley	170,800	20,738	26.0%
Bradford	463,900	30,849	15.3%
Sunderland	299,400	38,663	22.2%
Coventry (pilot study)	315,000	26,928	18.4%

29. After giving the final draft of the survey questionnaire further consideration, Walsall felt that they were no longer able to participate in the survey. Coventry were therefore incorporated as a full member of the sample to ensure representation from the West Midlands after the questionnaire had been piloted with them.

30. Selection of the survey areas was based on the regional spread and impact of unemployment and thus included regions of traditional unemployment (Manchester, Knowsley, Sunderland), areas of more recent unemployment (Bradford, and the pilot area of Coventry), inner-city areas exhibiting a wide variety of deprivation (Lambeth, Tower Hamlets) and, in contrast, an area of low unemployment (Harrow). Within these areas the different types of unemployment were and still are prominent, especially ethnic minority unemployment in Bradford and Lambeth and youth unemployment in Knowsley and Coventry. The high level of unemployment generally means that all types of unemployment prevail in each sample authority except in Harrow, where the scale is much less extensive.

31. Detailed economic profiles of the sample authorities are to be found at Appendix C. The results from the survey should be considered in the light of these profiles and the differences between authorities compared with the varying socio-economic conditions.

32. ***Data Collection*** Data was collected by four principal methods:-

(i) ***Review of Literature and Research*** — In the early stages this identified the subject area and those issues which were researchable. Later, written material and research (published and unpublished) were used as further evidence under the five service headings.

(ii) ***Self Completion Questionnaire*** — The major method of collecting data was a questionnaire completed by the participating authorities. This method was chosen to yield as much material as possible mobilising the resources within the sample authorities. This questionnaire was divided to correspond to the five specific service areas. There was also a more general sixth section for overall issues. The questionnaire was extensively piloted in Coventry.

The questions sought qualitative and quantitative information on trends in demand and provision of services and on the way in which service providers were encountering problems associated with unemployment.

(iii) ***Follow up Interviews*** — Some 52 interviews with 73 social services officers aimed to explore interesting responses to the questionnaire and to examine answers requiring further clarification. Informal interviewing techniques were used prompting discussion by reference to a response on the self-completion questionnaire or by a general question. The full range of social services personnel were interviewed from directors and officers in charge of children's homes and from field social workers to welfare rights officers.

(iv) ***Survey of Referrals*** — In view of the limited numerical data available from social services departments on employment status of clients it was decided to collect new data to fill an obvious gap in the data base. We obtained the co-operation of each sample authority to conduct a 'snapshot' survey of the employment/unemployment situation of all referrals dealt with by one social work area during a four-week period. Whilst we could not collect retrospective data we could collect comparative data by the use of a standard questionnaire. This section of the survey is described in further detail in Chapter 7.

Chapter 2
The Effect of Unemployment on Services for Physically and Mentally Handicapped People

Review of Literature and Research

1. Physically and mentally handicapped people are amongst those groups hit hardest by rising unemployment. Even before unemployment had begun to rise rapidly, Buckle had established that, of disabled people classified as employable, only half of the under-50s were at work and only 32% of those over 50.[1] Later, in 1974, a Department of Employment study showed that 13% of men and 10% of women registered as unemployed were disabled, a finding supported by Daniel's results at about the same time.[2,3] In 1981 an MSC study estimated 16% of the registered unemployed were disabled people and more recently still Michael White's study, 'Long-term Unemployment and Labour Markets', showed that amongst the long-term unemployed there is at least twice the prevalence of disability as occurs in the working population, even when age is taken into account.[4,5]

2. Such findings were further illustrated in Alan Walker's study of handicapped young people and the labour market.[6] This survey, commissioned by the Warnock Committee in 1975, took a sample of 18-year-olds from the 1958 National Child Development Study cohort. It found that handicapped people formed a severely disadvantaged minority, confined to a narrow range of jobs at low levels of skill; moreover, the percentage underemployed since school, i.e. employed for less than half the total time available for work since leaving school, was five times that of the non-handicapped.

3. The latter study provides a more eloquent statement of the problems of handicapped workers than can those based on samples of 'registered disabled'. Although the 1944 Disabled Persons (Employment) Act set up an employment placement service and quota system for the registered disabled, many are reluctant to register and participate in a scheme which labels them as significantly different from other people. Reluctance to register, plus the fact that no definition of 'disability' automatically means a person is handicapped in terms of employment, makes it very difficult to ascertain the numbers of unemployed handicapped people either on a national or a local basis.

4. In Lambeth, for example, when 400 people were registered as disabled and unemployed in 1982, a further 100 were known to Careers Officers as disabled young people looking for work and another 700 to Disablement Resettlement Offices in job centres. To this total of 1,200 had also to be added disabled women, unlikely to register for work, and many others with undefined health problems affecting their employment prospects. Thus it seems safe to say that, beyond those officially unemployed and disabled, are many others hidden away within the community.

5. Drawing on his own major survey in 1968-9 and the General Household Survey, Peter Townsend has also emphasised how the size of the disabled population of working age has been underestimated nationally.[7] Whereas the last Government estimate put this population at 1.29 million, Townsend calculates it to be nearer 3 million. The General Household Survey would seem to be the most reliable current estimate of this disabled population. It suggests that it has been increasing steadily over the past 10 years. It also suggests that over 16% of the population of working age is suffering from some kind of illness or disability which limits activities.[8] Given this lack of certainty, the OPCS proposal for a new full-scale survey of disabled people in 1985 is both appropriate and timely.

Evidence from the Survey

Places and Users

6. The institutions surveyed include local authority day centres for younger physically handicapped people, (i.e. those below retirement age), day centres, workshops and adult training centres (ATCs) for mentally handicapped people, sheltered workshops and sheltered industrial groups (SIGs). Day centres, workshops and ATCs have developed in piecemeal fashion over the last 50 years, variously sponsored by local authorities and voluntary agencies and with divergent aims. In many cases a division has grown up between those concerned with the development of life skills and socialisation and those concerned with industrial occupation and training. More recently it has been realised that individuals need both social, recreational and work-related skills in order to attempt to lead fuller, more independent lives. In the prevailing context of high unemployment, however, as this survey shows, these two goals are very difficult to achieve. Although the Manpower Services Commission has responsibility for policy on the operation of all the main services concerned with the employment, rehabilitation and training of disabled people, young disabled people look primarily to the local authority and to their careers service for guidance and placement. For those unable or too severely handicapped to obtain work, day centres and ATCs provide a wide range of activities. A survey of ATCs in the early 1970s showed that nearly two thirds of those attending were under 30 years and less than a tenth over 50; 80% were living in the family home and only 13% in hostels. Thus the majority of attenders at these centres were both young and dependent on their families. ATC places are limited, however, so much so that the Government has called for a substantial expansion in the number of ATC places.[9] Where these are not available most young people have no choice but to remain at home.

7. In the survey local authorities were asked for factual evidence on the numbers of places in the institutions concerned and their full or part-time users between 1979 and 1983, the average number of days in the week attended and numbers on their waiting lists. A further range of questions was then addressed to relevant officers concerned with open employment opportunities, the changing nature of the clients themselves and the types of programmes being provided. Follow-up interviews provided supplementary detail for evidence already given.

Centres for Physically Handicapped People

8. Information was provided by eight day centres for physically handicapped people. None of these reported any change at all in

the number of places available between 1979 and 1983 except for Harrow which opened a new centre in 1981. Four of these eight centres had many more users than places: in Coventry 100 places were occupied by 247 users attending on average two days a week; in Lambeth for 135 places there were 247 users in 1983; Knowsley with 60 places had 35 full-timers and 91 part-timers averaging 3-4 days a week and Harrow, with 65 places had 13 full-timers and 101 part-timers averaging 2-3 days a week.

9. It is true that physically handicapped people are sometimes more able than mentally handicapped people to occupy their time fruitfully with less guidance and therefore part-time attendance at day centres is often a suitable arrangement. However, these figures are still on a scale that suggests that the physically handicapped may be experiencing either overcrowding or undesirably shortened periods of attendance in these day centres, if not both. Subsequent interviews with officers in these centres confirmed that this was indeed the case, although authorities themselves did not keep evidence to show how far part-time attendance fell short of need.

10. On the other hand, two centres, one in Lambeth and another in Tower Hamlets, reported a shortfall in numbers. In Tower Hamlets a 90-place day centre had only 57 users, because the clients were severely handicapped and had transport difficulties. In Lambeth, both staff shortages and transport were cited as reasons for under-utilisation. Transport was also the problem creating waiting lists in Lambeth and Bradford. Most physically handicapped people are dependent on specialised transport and it is apparent that in all the local authorities surveyed this was in short supply.

11. Apart from Lambeth and Bradford no authority appeared to have a waiting list. It is clear, however, that this is in itself no indication of satisfied demand. In general, social services departments do not keep waiting lists for services where the prospects of admission are remote. Interviews revealed the several policies used to avoid waiting lists building up. Part-time attendance was the most obvious method, but beyond that there were simple refusals to take, for example, elderly applicants who were redirected to other establishments which were more 'social' in nature. Furthermore, social workers were reluctant to refer individuals to establishments already known to be full and searched for alternatives. Although all the authorities when asked denied that they rationed places, what has been described is a form of indirect rationing.

12. For many physically handicapped people the only alternative to a place in a day centre is to stay at home. This often appears to be the course of action taken. In the past parents have seen day centres as a last resort, an attitude slow to change. In areas of high unemployment, like Knowsley for example, young handicapped people also often stay at home because it is too much of an effort for their families to prepare them for the journey to and from the centre. The handicapped person in a family where the other adults are unemployed may actually be the only one to have a structured day and a timetable which it is emotionally difficult for his or her parents to accept.

Centres for Mentally Handicapped People

13. The response to the survey from centres for mentally handicapped people was in considerable contrast to that for the physically handicapped; several new centres had been opened, almost all the centres were full and some waiting lists were reported. However, it should be noted that not all the centres in the authorities concerned responded and that no simple distinction can be drawn between them and those for the physically handicapped. Mentally handicapped people are often physically handicapped as well and in some centres mentally and physically handicapped individuals are mixed together. In all, information was provided by 19 centres. Four of these were new within the period covered by the survey(1979-83) — three in Coventry and one in Sunderland — and places had also been increased in other centres in Knowsley, Sunderland, Manchester and Bradford. Virtually all were full, with their users attending five days a week and only a very few on a part-time basis. Again in contrast, several reported waiting lists in 1983 — 8 on a waiting list in Knowsley, 9 in Harrow and 14 and 19 at two separate centres in Bradford. The fear was voiced repeatedly that these lists would be growing over the next few years, a point to be discussed in detail later.

Other Facilities

14. Other establishments on which information was sought were sheltered workshops and sheltered industrial groups (SIGs). Whilst the 1944 Disabled Persons (Employment) Act encouraged the expansion of sheltered employment, it has been noted that since then there have been few related developments of any significance. Sheltered workshops are still devoted to manufacturing or packaging work although this has been a declining sector of the British economy for some years.[10] It was not surprising to find that sheltered workshops and SIGs were thin on the ground. Coventry has one sheltered workshop for the physically handicapped, an industrial therapy unit attended by the older disabled who use the activity primarily for maintaining self-image and by younger physically handicapped people who are encouraged to go to the unit twice weekly to give routine and discipline to their week. It was reported that some of the latter group did not like going there and not surprisingly regarded their payment of 40p daily as a pittance. In Coventry also two industrial enclaves for the mentally handicapped, employing 30 and 45 people respectively, were developed, the one in 1983 and the other in 1981. Both were with packaging firms and both have had to close due to the problems of the firms involved. Only three other sheltered workshops were identified, in Sunderland, Manchester and Bradford. The general impression given was of a lack of cohesive provision and planning amongst the authorities for sheltered work. This is not surprising, given that sheltered employment is expensive to set up and run and sheltered workshops run at a loss. Where profitability becomes the aim, as in some workshops, including those of Remploy, only workers with very minor handicaps can be considered for employment and the main object of employing disabled persons is only partially achieved.

15. This preliminary evidence on available places and their users in day centres, ATCs and sheltered employment suggests that demand for these services is not being adequately met. *Overcrowding, understaffing, lack of transport, lack of sheltered working environments and waiting lists are just some of the problems being faced by physically and mentally handicapped people attending or seeking to attend these institutions.* Subsequent findings show that these problems are being exacerbated by the current high levels of unemployment.

Employment Opportunities and Changing Policies

16. A series of questions was put to relevant officers as part of the survey, to gain further quantitative evidence as well as professional opinion, on the movements of both physically and mentally handicapped people in and out of open employment and local authority responses. Although some centres have clients too severely handicapped ever to be capable of open employment, most do have some individuals who would have been employable in better times or who today could work with some initial help. Officers estimated that anywhere between 4% and 20% of clients could be considered as possible employees.

17. The first of these questions focused on the numbers of clients moving into open employment from centres between 1978-9 and 1982-3. *An almost uniform picture of declining opportunity emerged.* Of Bradford's three social education centres with employable clients, the first could report only one client moving into open employment — one who has since been made redundant. The second could report no movement at all and the third had evidence of only three placements, two of whom have since left work. In Knowsley four people out of a total of 17 leaving the social centre for the physically handicapped in the first half of 1984 found employment and about two a year were moving out of the workshop. In Coventry a few clients were able to move on to Remploy — a total in fact of three over the past five years — but no other openings were available. Harrow, the area with the least unemployment, reported a total of 37 clients placed from their ATC between 1970 and 1976, with only two failing and returning, but only one client was placed between 1978 and 1983. Lambeth and Tower Hamlets offered no figures, but both regarded employment opportunities for handicapped people as at an all-time low. The most precise and telling figures came from Manchester and Sunderland. They illustrate clearly the shrinking employment opportunities for handicapped people, many more of whom than previously must now look to local authority services as their sole means of daytime occupation and activity. (See Table 1.)

18. Authorities were also asked if clients formerly in open employment were returning to centres they had previously attended and if the proportion of new entrants capable of open employment was changing. Bradford, Manchester and Lambeth all reported some

Table 1 — Numbers of Mentally Handicapped People from ATCs Entering Employment

	1978–79	1979–80	1980–81	1981–82	1982–83
Manchester ATCs					
Nos. into open employment	5	3	1	1	0
Sunderland ATC					
Nos. into open employment	6	10	20	0	0

returners. Harrow pointed out that such returners would not, however, be considered as day centre candidates having been in open employment but as simply 'unemployed'. Sunderland remarked that the trend in returners had in fact been more apparent when unemployment was lower and more of a stigma. Now feelings of isolation and stigma have decreased because of mass unemployment and pressures to find a work substitute, such as that provided in an ATC, were not so intense any longer.

19. The extent to which new, handicapped clients were seen as employable was hedged with qualifications. At one end of the spectrum there is no doubt that many centres are now receiving more severely handicapped individuals than ever before, both as a result of advances in medical science prolonging life and as a result of dehospitalisation policies. The setting up of special units for such individuals, with a necessarily high staff/client ratio, is proving very problematic where funds are restricted. Such individuals would never be expected to work, and all efforts are aimed at improving their quality of life.

20. At the other extreme, centres are experiencing the attendance of more able clients who previously would have been in employment. In Sunderland, for example, an increase of more able young people was recorded between 1978 and 1982. This influx has temporarily slackened, however, due it would seem to three factors which were of concern and interest in all the authorities, namely the raising of the school leaving age for those in special schools to 19 years by the 1981 Education Act, the increase of Youth Training Schemes and the development of further education courses in local colleges.

Handicapped People and Education

21. There is some evidence to suggest that more mentally handicapped teenagers are staying on at school after 16.

Table 2 — Mentally Handicapped Teenagers Staying at School After 16 Years

	1979	1980	1981	1982	1983
Coventry	11	17	16	22	25
Knowsley	1	2	11	17	14

In Coventry the numbers have almost doubled and in Knowsley the numbers have risen too, although part of the rise in this instance was due to four profoundly handicapped people staying on because there were no ATC places for them. Other authorities confirmed similar patterns. There is a lack of evidence on what is happening to the physically handicapped. In Coventry numbers of physically handicapped teenagers staying on after 16 years seem actually to have fallen, a fact put down to lack of facilities. In Lambeth the case would seem to be even worse, with one school for the physically handicapped now closed and the other having lost its sixth form. No evidence emerged to suggest that, in compensation, physically handicapped children and older teenagers are being successfully integrated into normal education.

22. Several authorities reported teaching schemes for the handicapped being set up by local colleges. For example, from Harrow some mentally handicapped 16 to 19 year-olds are now attending the Oxford College of Further Study; from Knowsley some are going to the local college; in Tower Hamlets Hackney College is offering placements for 19 to 22 year-olds; and in Coventry Tilehill College is now taking 10 mentally handicapped students for a full college year. Many saw these developments as very encouraging with much to be gained by the students. Fears were voiced, however, that this development was sometimes more a part of a college's own survival strategy than a response to a social need. Courses were also criticised as inappropriate, the education offered was felt to lack direction and was unrelated except very indirectly to future employment, and sometimes colleges did not provide the social services with adequate feedback on courses taken and student performance. An associated problem frequently raised is that increased education raises parental expectations for their handicapped children's future but without fitting the children for the job market in any tangible way. As education finishes, so the handicapped are faced with staying at home or going to ATCs 'as a last resort'.

23. A special school in Tower Hamlets has provided the following illustrations:

> 'The pupils at this school are severely handicapped and for many years the prospect of finding open employment on leaving school has been quite unviable. This situation arises principally as a result of the nature of the young adults, handicap and retardation of their general intellectual ability levels and social and emotional development levels. At the age of 19 they are simply not ready to take up employment but with continued education after the age of 19 it is likely that some would, in later years, have achieved the necessary skills and levels of independence that would facilitate the readiness for employment if such employment was available.
>
> The current picture of school leavers in the last year is composed of 5 young adults, 2 of whom joined the Hackney College of Further Education Course, 2 joined the Adult Social Education Centre, and one remained at home as a result of parental choice. Prior to leaving school these young adults have experienced a curriculum designed to meet their specific needs as a result of which there has been much concentration on the development of life skills and leisure skills where the intention is to foster maximum personal independence and integration into the local community.'

24. The general opinion held by local authority officers is that so far *educational developments have done no more than give centres for the physically and mentally handicapped a temporary respite*. There are very few employment prospects for handicapped youngsters once they have run the gamut of these courses and already some of these youngsters are arriving at the day centres. In Harrow, for example, where employment opportunities are better than elsewhere, the ATC is now full as a result of the influx of the profoundly handicapped from hospital and school leavers from the local special school. This ATC has never been full before and now has nine on its waiting list. Also the Shaftesbury School has made three referrals of mild cases although none have ever come from this school to the social services before. Since there will be 45 school leavers coming to Harrow's ATC over the next three years the problem is now seen as acute.

25. From responses received it is also clear that centres are having to turn away those with mild mental handicaps. There is no future for these teenagers, but to join the dole queue. They are right at the bottom of the employment ladder and yet have no priority for social services support at a time when the sort of jobs they used to do are fast disappearing. In Coventry, for example, 157 ESN(M) teenagers left school in 1983. Three of these found employment, only one of whom is now still at work.

The Work Ethic Versus Creative Activities

26. Declining employment prospects seem to be making more handicapped young people than before turn to day centres and ATCs for support. They are also resulting in young people remaining in centres for longer periods than before with an inevitable lack of turnover and places. Such pressures on staff and resources may reasonably be expected to create changes in the nature of the work undertaken in centres and the regimes applied. Much in this survey has suggested that this is indeed the case, although the general picture is by no means clear or uniform. It is backed moreover by the development of criticism of the 'work-centred' approach and the encouragement of creative pursuits and social skills for their own sake that occurred well before the impact of unemployment was felt.

27. *The majority of centres reported a shift towards creative and rehabilitation activity, partly because this was felt to be better for individuals and partly because it was more appropriate in the present economic climate in which it was unrealistic to expect handicapped people to find jobs.* In Tower Hamlets, for example, one day centre reported that seven years ago most clients would have been working either in the woodwork room or on packaging; now about 60% are thus involved, the other 40% receiving further education and social training. However, when short of staff, more clients are put back to work activities. In Sunderland, where the prime objective used to be open employment, social education is now the aim. This however involves a broader range of staff and greater teaching skills than previously were necessary. This is particularly the case where social education involves any element of deinstitutionalisation, taking individuals, for example, out into the community on shopping exercises or on holiday and helping them to mingle normally. *Creative and rehabilitation activities are thus expensive in terms of both* *staff and other resources and likely to suffer when available finance is limited.*

28. There is ample evidence that above all else, however, young handicapped people still want a job and give surprising support to the idea of the work ethic. In Knowsley where youth unemployment is so high, the handicapped young are said to be prepared to give almost anything to have a job. This attitude lends strength to those who still put faith in the sheltered workshop approach, the original conception of which was to train disabled people for open employment by educating them in the discipline of work. Though much has been criticised in workshop activity the importance to young people of work-related skills is unquestionable. Workshops are able to produce labour-intensive goods which are uneconomical commercially and thus they are able to find work in the gaps remaining in the market. In Tower Hamlets, for example, the woodworkshop mends and paints park benches and provides basic school apparatus like test-tube racks, for the GLC and ILEA. Where authorities like Bradford, however, rely on conducting the labour-intensive parts of factory production, the closure of big factories has caused considerable difficulties. In this sort of situation the costs of running a workshop depend on the amount of contract work and any shortfall of revenue over expenditure has to be met by the local authority.

29. It is the cost of workshops at a time of economic stringency that militates against their improvement and expansion; this is in spite of MSC capitation grants which are supposed to cover costs. In Knowsley a successful carpentry workshop in a day centre manufactures trophies, benches, desks, chairs and Welsh dressers and finds a ready market. But plans to turn this into a full sheltered workshop a couple of years ago came to nothing because the local authority felt the cost was too high. It is this that is currently deterring local authorities from implementing any plans they might have had for developing sheltered work environments. In response to the survey, only Coventry reported having committed itself to the development of SIGs and to have put money aside for this purpose.

30. The major work still being done by mentally handicapped people within the day centres is packaging. Coventry and Tower Hamlets reported no shortage of packaging work. Packaging is costly and difficult to automate and much is best done manually, especially if there is a source of cheap labour. One manager reported turning away several thousand pounds worth of work in September 1984. It is the 'cheap labour' aspect of this activity, however, that so many find disturbing. The pittance paid bears no comparison to what could be earned in open employment. Mentally handicapped people are very good at monotonous jobs, not losing concentration nor, once trained in a particular activity, deviating from instructions. Recently, for example, a food-canning company, which had problems with high turnover of labour on very repetitive work, successfully recruited mentally retarded people from a nearby ATC. These workers did not see the work as repetitive and used their capabilities to the full.[11] Such opportunities, allowing mentally handicapped people to participate properly in open employment, are, however, rare.

31. The main issue here is probably not the capability of the mentally handicapped to work but finance. Poor remuneration is a deterrent to work and it can result in a reduction of benefits to a level at which working becomes impracticable. In this case it may well be the handicapped person's family that discourages searching out employment opportunities or taking them up.

32. This discussion has tried to illustrate the dilemma faced by those organising appropriate activities for handicapped people. Developing creativity and life skills is recognised as tremendously valuable and many efforts are being made in this direction but the acquisition of work skills, making possible eventual independent participation in the wider community, is also very important to physically and mentally handicapped people. Officers are now faced therefore with trying to pursue these two goals simultaneously. *Their work is bedevilled at the current time both by the shortfall of staff and resources and by the knowledge that the handicapped at a time of high unemployment are very unlikely to be able to put any work skills to good use.*

Creating Work Opportunities for Handicapped People

33. Finally the survey asked authorities if any regular arrangements were made with local employers aimed at providing employment for the handicapped and whether such arrangements had declined or become more difficult to operate in recent years. Responses were generally negative and pessimistic. In Harrow and Manchester there were no arrangements, in Knowsley earlier contacts with the employers were said to have disappeared. In Sunderland staff at the ATC had liaised in the past with the local DRO and when any suitable vacancies arose in open employment a panel was convened to select clients to put forward for interview. A mark of the total lack of open employment opportunities for mentally handicapped clients attending this ATC can be seen in the fact that this panel has not met since about 1980. Several authorities also remarked that local employers were neither forthcoming nor helpful in trying to place handicapped people within their plants or offices.

34. In Tower Hamlets and Bradford, although contacts were few and far between, MENCAP's Pathway scheme was making some headway. In Tower Hamlets the Pathway officer has recently helped to place three mentally handicapped people, one in Tesco's, one in Sainsbury's and one in a part-time gardening job, suggesting more openings than many would credit possible. Such efforts are time-consuming and expensive, however, and clearly in most cases local authority resources are not adequate to support them. In Bradford, the Pathway scheme seemed to have met with less success: from one social education centre it has placed one person, from a second, none, from a third only one and from a fourth only one who had since left employment. The fact that six people are now being assessed by Pathway in Bradford does still, however, indicate a little hope. In Coventry the newly appointed Employment Promotions Officer has been negotiating with firms for new placements. Initial successes are encouraging with recent placements having been negotiated with Sainsbury, Asda and Jaguar. It is clear however that this is uphill work which requires considerable resources behind it as well as the commitment and co-operation of local firms if it is to meet with any success.

35. There is no doubt that authorities would like to establish greater working opportunities for handicapped people in the wider environment and to this end many small schemes have got underway. Few however are of the size and scope necessary to have a real impact on such a difficult situation. One noteworthy major project is the Lambeth ACCORD, an EEC project which has been set up to co-ordinate services and community initiatives in Lambeth and thus increase the opportunities for disabled people to gain employment and social integration. Total funding for this centre was set at £96,710 for 1983-84 with a net cost to the social services of over £20,000. Such schemes do not come cheaply. This project has three main parts, involving firstly co-ordination of the efforts of all the agencies involved in the economic rehabilitation of handicapped people and the services which support or facilitate employment; secondly a self-help resource centre for disabled people; and thirdly a work introduction centre. Since the centre has only just been established, however, it is not possible as yet to give any details of its progress.

Conclusion

36. From a broad range of information the impression gained has been one of severely strained resources beginning to adjust to the hostile economic climate of the 1980s. Employment opportunities for handicapped people have declined in all the authorities surveyed and centres are experiencing the attendance of more able clients who previously would have been out at work. Day centres and ATCs are frequently overcrowded or understaffed and their clients are frustrated by waiting lists and transport difficulties. Although more handicapped teenagers are staying on at school after 16, taking up new places in colleges of education, or going on MSC schemes, the respite thus given to day centres and ATCs is temporary. Handicapped young people cannot find employment and are expected to come to the day centres and ATCs in increasing numbers in the very near future. At a time of economic stringency, meeting the needs of these young people, as well as those of older handicapped people, for creative activities, the acquisition of social skills and, in addition, training for employment, is very difficult. It demands levels of provision well beyond those currently available.

37. Attempts at job creation can help, but so far these have been limited, with finance a major problem. Even the costs of increasing the traditional form of provision (both capital and revenue) are daunting and the experimental approaches, as in the ACCORD scheme, are probably beyond the financial capacity of most of the authorities surveyed — especially when other competing demands are considered, including the reduction of public expenditure. Such a reduction will increase the chances of failure by local authorities to meet the needs of mentally and physically handicapped people and will in turn put more pressure on families whose capacity to survive may depend on traditional forms of support.

Chapter 3
Employment Prospects Of Children In Care

Review Of Literature And Research

1. This chapter focuses on the employment situation of children and young people in the care of local authorities and the impact this has on the need for social services support. Our hypotheses are that increasing numbers of children in care are unable to find paid employment and that this has consequences for the work load and type of care provided by social services departments. This may include an extension of the period of stay in residential care beyond statutory limits as a result of decreased ability of young people to move towards independence.

2. *We know that children in care, or leaving care, are more prone to unemployment than the youth population as a whole.* The Leaving Care Project at the University of Leeds[1] is currently examining both the employment prospects of young people who have left care and the employment expectations and experiences of a group of young people in care. This project has uncovered extra difficulties for this group in finding employment compared with the majority of young people. Burgess (1981)[2] surveyed the employment situation of young people in the care of the St Christopher's Fellowship. Although this was a small sample (43) he found that the young people in the group encountered greater difficulty in obtaining employment, or gaining the necessary qualifications to secure employment, and are less able to cope with the emotional problems posed by unemployment, than the youth population at large.

Burgess identified the importance of employment to the transition of young people in care to independence and stable adulthood.

3. Research in progress at the Tavistock Institute of Human Relations has revealed that 53% of a sample of young people aged 17 to 24 who have left care were unemployed. This compares with 18% unemployed in the 16 to 25 age population nationally. This proportion had declined only marginally to 42% some 6 to 9 months later for the same group of young people.[3]

4. Official DHSS statistics reveal similar trends. Figures on children leaving care, for example, demonstrate a reducing proportion of children leaving care because they became self-supporting, or went to live with family or friends. The proportion in this category leaving care fell from 62% in 1977 to 53% in 1982.[4] DHSS figures also reveal that an increasing proportion of young people in care are aged 16 and over,[5] increasing from 23.1% in 1977 to 25.5% in 1982.

5. There are few research findings indicating a relationship between unemployment in society or families in general, and the incidence of children coming into care. Research by Frank Loughran,[6] has attempted to correlate the incidence of children entering care with rates of unemployment. This relationship strengthened through the late 1970s and into the 80s but has levelled off in recent years. Strathclyde Regional Council,[7] have surveyed the impact of unemployment on services throughout their authority. They report that 70% of children in care originate from families with unemployed parents. The regional rate of unemployment was 13.9% at the time of the survey.

6. A phenomenon which was well documented at a time of higher unemployment was the high job turnover of children in care. Several studies identified this as a common feature among this group. A more recent study by Porter[8] identified it as a feature of a group of 20 young people who have left care, 10 of whom secured some form of full-time work. Porter concludes that this tendency to high job turnover can only further disadvantage young people in care, or formerly in care, in the job market.

7. It is likely therefore that as the number of young people in care who are unemployed increases so does the pressure on social services provision increase as follows:-

(i) Children remain in care longer, stretching residential and foster-care resources.

(ii) More young people are likely to require 'after care' provision under S27 of the 1980 Child Care Act as they find it increasingly difficult to cope after leaving care.

> 'Young people in care need the stability of a job if they are to make a success of their transition to adult life. The more they are out of work, the less experience they will be able to offer as an attribute when applying for a job.' (Burgess,[2] p69.)

(iii) The difficulty of finding jobs for children in care creates increased work for residential and field social workers in helping young people find work. As Burgess[2] reports:

> 'In helping young people in care who are leaving school, residential staff face a multiplicity of tasks, preparatory and advisory; a great deal rests on their judgement, interest, and ability. School leavers in care have to compete for scarce jobs with other young people in the knowledge that failure will not be cushioned by kinship support. Their relative chances will be enhanced where they receive the most appropriate advice on job opportunities and preparatory experiences and above all access to the most suitable local labour markets . . . This gap between provision and need must be filled, in the first instance, by the residential worker. Such a statement is not intended as a demand that residential staff should take on the role of job advisers or placement agencies. Rather they are ideally placed to fulfil the vital role of helping young people in care establish their occupational identity.'

(iv) The increased presence of young people in and around community homes during the daytime, due to their unemployment, increases the staffing requirements and the difficulty of caring tasks. Many homes are staffed on the assumption that most children will not be present during the day.

(v) Unemployment has a greater psychological impact on young people in care than young people in general, increasing their need for social work support.

> 'It is difficult for young people to convince themselves that failure to secure a place in the labour market is not necessarily a reflection on their worth or potential.
> Unemployment is demoralizing enough for those young people whose backgrounds have given them every reason to feel personally secure and confident. Those who . . . are disadvantaged in one or multiple ways may find themselves simply unable to cope and may . . . turn against a society which, as they see it patently has no interest in them.' (Gulbenkian Foundation, 1979)[9]

Findings From Survey

8. The quantitative evidence on this subject was patchy. The qualitative evidence was however both extensive and consistent. There were only three available numerical indicators which we considered could demonstrate points raised earlier in the chapter. These were: (i) the number of children in care aged 16+; (ii) the proportion of children in care not working; (iii) the trend in young people requiring continued support after leaving care. Social services departments should be able to provide quantitative data on these three indicators but, with no obvious need to retain such data in practice, records are not aggregated or presented in these convenient forms even though the information has been collected.

(ii) The Number of Children in Care Aged 16 and Over

9. As demonstrated earlier, the national figures show an increasing proportion of children aged 16 and over in care. Evidence from interviews with residential social workers suggests that children are staying in children's homes to older ages and the average age of those in homes is increasing. This is not reflected in the survey figures from the sample authorities (Table 1). This is because these give the total number in care wherever placed and do not, unfortunately, distinguish numbers in community homes.

Table 1 — Numbers of Children in Care aged 16 and over and Proportion of all Children in Care[10]

	YEAR (as at 31 March)				
AUTHORITY	1979	1980	1981	1982	1983
Sunderland	52 (8%)	131 (22%)	126 (23%)	131 (27%)	80 (18%)
Knowsley	154 (22%)	176 (24%)	162 (22%)	133 (22%)	133 (22%)
Lambeth	454 (29%)	462 (30%)	374 (26%)	359 (28%)	346 (29%)
Tower Hamlets	247(N/A)	238 (24%)	120 (13%)	206 (25%)	198 (25%)
Harrow	42 (25%)	57 (34%)	49 (33%)	34 (25%)	33 (30%)
Bradford	380 (23%)	389 (24%)	395 (23%)	394 (26%)	350 (25%)
Coventry	176 (22%)	190 (23%)	185 (22%)	U/A	196 (26%)
Manchester	531 (24%)	538 (25%)	552 (21%)	562 (31%)	472 (26%)

10. The data from the sample is variable. The numbers tell us little, but the proportions of children in care aged 16 and over appear to confirm the national trend showing a slight increase.

Two authorities showed a notable increase in the number of young people aged 16 and over in care, Sunderland and Coventry — the latter an area noted for youth unemployment.

(ii) The Impact of Unemployment on Community Homes and Fostering Homes

11. Numerical data collected by social services departments which could indicate the numbers of children working are the records of financial contributions towards board and lodging by children in care. All children in care aged 16 and over are required by law to contribute towards their maintenance. Working children have always had to do this, and it has more recently become a requirement for children on benefits. The size of contribution differs between those working and those not working, and data could be available from finance sections of social services departments. However, social services departments tend not to retain this data retrospectively and therefore little information was obtained from the sample authorities. Such evidence as was available was inconclusive.

12. *The evidence from interviews however demonstrated that residential social workers have been alarmed at the increase in unemployment amongst children in care, which is significantly higher than for young people generally.* So much so that in those authorities where unemployment is highest, children in community homes have no chance of getting a job unless they are quite exceptionally talented.

(a) *The Employment Situation in Individual Homes*

13. Many officers in charge of community homes were able to provide details of the change in employment prospects and the disproportionate effect unemployment has on children in care.

> 'From September 1980 to September 1983 31 girls left the hostel; 17 became unemployed, 8 became employed (including YTS) and 6 entered full time education.' (An officer in charge of a home for girls in Bradford)

14. A fostering officer in Bradford reported that up to seven years ago he could not remember a child in care for whom a job could not be obtained. Even now young people in foster homes seem to be as likely to obtain jobs as young people not in care. Children in community homes, on the other hand, seem to be less successful than the average young person from the community. For example, he reported that of the 9 children in one home who have left school this summer, 7 have no work and little prospect of obtaining any.

15. Similarly in Coventry heads of homes report that finding jobs, other than YTS, is virtually impossible. Only one or two have gained employment.

16. An officer in charge of a large home in Manchester demonstrated the changing opportunities for young people in care. Five years ago most young people in care pursued a trade; two years ago YOP and then a reasonable chance of a job; now it is YTS followed by nothing. Three larger homes in Manchester put figures together showing that in the last three years only 15% of those eligible found regular work and half of these did so only through family connections.

17. Even in Harrow children in care are finding it more difficult to obtain jobs in recent years. Numbers reported to be obtaining work are small; a percentage may have found jobs easily in the past but it is now the norm for young people in residential care not to get jobs on leaving school.

18. In Tower Hamlets the only jobs available to young people in care, if at all, are manual or clerical. Employment prospects have declined significantly. One officer in charge of a home in Tower Hamlets reports that of 8 children who have left the home over the last four years 6 did not find jobs.

19. In Lambeth the present outlook for children in care is similarly gloomy. One officer in charge of a home reported that the only prospect on leaving school is a YTS scheme. Another officer in charge of a home reported that 3-4 years ago a number of young people were able to find employment. Now people are unemployed for about 3-4 years with no work experience. About half a dozen people in the last 10 years had been able to find work from this particular home. In their independence units for young people about to leave care, out of 10 placed in the last year only one was employed.

20. The situation in Knowsley is extreme:

> 'Over the last three years, no child has been successful in gaining permanent work. Only training schemes have been available — for a limited period of time.' (Officer in charge of a community home)

21. Another officer in charge of a home in Knowsley reported that the last young person in the home to get a permanent job was in 1980.

22. Similarly in a home in Sunderland between 1981 and 1984 not one child has found employment on leaving school, other than on Government schemes. In another home of five children who have left, none has obtained employment.

23. *It appears from this evidence that a significant majority of young people in residential care, or who have left residential care, are unemployed, 50% and more in many cases, and in some of the authorities with the worst youth unemployment rates nearly all children in residential care aged 16 and over are unemployed.*

(b) *Arrangements with Local Employers*

24. *Further evidence of the trend in employment opportunities for children in care is demonstrated by a decline in arrangements between local authorities and local employers to place children in care in their employment.* Such arrangements were formerly quite common and a great benefit to young people in care who were otherwise disadvantaged in the job market. Employers would see this as a philanthropic gesture and take these young people 'under their wing'. The recession has hit local employers and led to a reduction or complete suspension of such arrangements in many areas. In many authorities in the sample, the only special arrangements they now have for children in care are with the careers office and job centre.

(c) *Types of Jobs Young People in Care are Obtaining*

25. Another indication of the decline in job opportunities of children in care is the type and quality of jobs obtained by those who find work. We asked officers in charge of homes what sort of jobs, if any, young people in their home were obtaining compared to 3-5 years ago. *The trend identified was of declining quality from trades, office and semi-skilled work for many 5-10 years ago, to unskilled work if any at all nowadays.* The majority of young people in care in the sample authorities now enter YTS. Many young people in care used to enter apprenticeships, now there are rarely such opportunities. In Manchester for example, there has been a general drift away from 'trade' and clerically based jobs, including apprenticeships, towards jobs which are one or more of: (a) temporary, (b) unskilled and (c) low-paid. Those young people who might previously have filled the more menial posts through lack of ability are now finding themselves permanently unemployed.

(d) *The Effects of Increased Unemployment on Children's Homes*

26. *The majority of officers in charge of homes stated that unemployment in recent years had led to an increased presence of young people aged 16 and over in and around community homes during the working day.* This has created significant problems for, and extra pressure on, staff. The most notable illustrations come from those units in the sample described as 'working boys/girls homes' where 5-10 years ago it was possible to close the home down, unstaffed, from 9 am to 5 pm in the confident expectation that all residents would, or could, work. Now the majority of these residents are not working and require attention during the day. This has the following consequences:-

27. ***Effect on Routines and Role of Staff*** — Traditional staff routines and rosters were designed at a time when it was reasonable to expect that all the young people in a home would be either at school or work with minimal staff cover during the day. Some officers in charge of homes report that extra staff have been recruited to cope with this, whilst the majority have had to spread their existing resources more thinly. *In reality there is a need for more staff in community homes to cover the extra daytime pressure resulting from the presence of unemployed young people.*

28. The effect on staffing rosters and remuneration was illustrated by an officer in charge in Sunderland:

> 'Children leaving school are in the home all day until they eventually find a scheme. This means that we cannot repay time owing to staff during the day whereas we could previously do this. Time owed must now be paid at the overtime rate.'

29. Five to ten years ago it was reasonable to expect that young people aged 16 plus would be either at work or education during the day and with their peers in the evening. *Now there are large tracts of the working day which young people need to fill often requiring the assistance and creative resources of staff.* Furthermore recreational activities in the evening are less accessible to young people whose only income is from supplementary benefit.

30. The occupying of time is more difficult for young people in care than for most other young people, given their lesser ability to be self-directing and propensity towards difficult behaviour. A head of home in Tower Hamlets sums up the experience in community homes:

> 'The increased presence of children during the daytime has many implications for the home and its staff. The fact that children have "nothing" to do or look forward to except signing on days means that they look for entertainment etc within the home. They become increasingly difficult to motivate and also make it difficult to maintain those in work who also want to stay at home rather than get up and go to work. Of course it also means that staff are necessary during the day to work with these children'.

Officers in charge in other authorities report similar experiences.

31. *Unemployment builds upon existing problems and social disadvantages. Officers in charge reported that the boredom and pressure of unemployment can have significant effects on the behaviour and morale of young people in care.* This is often exacerbated by their diminished ability to cope with such pressure coupled with limited support in the form of family relations. In addition many young people in care already exist on the edge of (or are more vulnerable to) criminality or already have criminal histories. Unemployment creates the opportunity and impetus to slip into criminality, glue sniffing and drug abuse. The problems begin with difficulty getting young people out of bed in the morning as they have no motivation, and thereafter maintaining a discipline during the day. As an officer in charge of a home in Bradford put it — when young people get bored they start to get into trouble.

32. *In the absence of work opportunities, staff of community homes are having to help find work for young people in care. Officers in charge throughout the country reported increased staff activity helping young people to apply for jobs, seeking opportunities, preparing for interviews, attending careers offices and job centres in addition to general encouragement and support.* Staff are also increasingly involved in helping young people cope with unemployment through helping them 'sign-on' and claim benefit. Some officers in charge reported that preparation for unemployment commences before leaving school in those areas where there is little prospect of finding work.

33. *Disincentives to Work* —There was some evidence from a few authorities in the sample that disincentives for children in care to find work have increased as unemployment has worsened. First, this arises from peer group pressure in areas where the majority of young people in homes are unemployed. Residential social workers reported that any young people who found work were under pressure to give it up and conform with the rest. Also, the requirement to pay contributions towards their board and lodgings often means that young people can be almost as well off financially on supplementary benefit as in low paid work, and still be able to hang around with friends, the majority of whom are unemployed also. Evidence of these disincentive effects was restricted to those authorities with the highest levels of employment e.g. Bradford and Sunderland.

34. There was also much evidence throughout the survey from both social workers and young people in care of a negative attitude towards youth training schemes on the part of young people. Most young people in care have not experienced YTS leading to real employment; a significant proportion do not even wish to take up an offer of work experience. At best YTS is viewed by young people in care as better than unemployment but not a substitute for real employment. At worst young people have the attitude, as expressed by a social worker in Bradford: 'Why should they go on a YTS and get £25 a week when they can stay in bed and get almost as much on the dole?'

35. ***Contrast Between Foster Homes and Community Homes*** — Evidence was collected from social workers and officers dealing with the fostering of children as well as those responsible for children in community homes. The picture to emerge was that although young people boarded out were likely to suffer the consequences of unemployment more than those youngsters living with their natural parents, they tend to suffer less than those in community homes. This was not always the case but the greater stability, regularity and wide range of contacts including those with adults tended to help youngsters cope with unemployment better and also assist them in finding and obtaining work.

36. ***Disadvantage in the Job Market*** — *In comparison with young people in general, children in care suffer a distinct disadvantage in the job market.* One source of this disadvantage is the reluctance on the part of employers to employ children in care particularly when they have an extensive choice of potential employees. Part of the reason for this is their misconception or fear that all children in care have criminal tendencies. Another reason is that children in care tend to have lower educational and social skills than young people as a whole, as would be expected from those with unstable and insecure backgrounds. For example, officers in charge of homes reported that employers have a ready pool of young people with sound educational and social backgrounds. Regrettably, young people leaving care have often failed to achieve their full potential in school, not necessarily because of innate lack of ability, but frequently as a result of associated social/emotional factors. Consequently in a contracting job market, such children are further disadvantaged. We spoke to young people in Bradford who had been in care and are now in the Bradford After Care Group. In practice they found that if they let potential employers know they were, or had been, in care they were less likely to take them on. Consequently young people disguise the fact that they are in care. In Bradford employers are looking only for people with experience, qualifications or prepared to work as YTS or on low wages. Young people in care can generally offer none of these.

(iii) The Impact of Unemployment on Children Leaving Care

37. Under section 27 of the Child Care Act 1980, social services departments have an enabling power to assist young people who have left care and are in need of material or social assistance. This help is frequently financial, e.g. helping with college fees, furniture, rent etc, all of which reflect the lack of money from other sources including employment. Some authorities are able to provide data on the number of young people who have received support under section 27.

Table 2 — Number of Young People Receiving Support Under Section 27 of the 1980 Child Care Act

AUTHORITY	YEAR 1978/79	1979/80	1980/81	1981/82	1982/83
Sunderland	4	7	7	5	13
Knowsley	NIL	NIL	3	4	7
Lambeth	U/A	U/A	47	28	29
Tower Hamlets	93	145	117	126	135
Harrow	3	4	U/A	U/A	U/A
Manchester	22	23	16	18	31

No information was available from Coventry and Bradford.

38. *With the exception of Lambeth all authorities demonstrate an increase in after-care support under section 27 between 1978/9 and 1982/3.* One cause of this trend may be the financial difficulties faced by young people living in the community on supplementary benefit. Section 27 money is used in the most extreme cases to help with rent and heating bills.

39. However, much of the after-care support for children leaving, or who have left, care is not officially recorded under section 27 support. Much of the help is qualitative involving residential and field social workers. It was clear that such work with young people had been increasing in all the authorities in the sample in recent years. *Most officers in charge of homes and fostering officers report that it was becoming more difficult for young people in care to move towards independence.* Problems associated with transition out of care are increasing and the numbers of young people unable to cope on their own have been increasing. It was also possible for social services officers to identify the causes primarily as financial, isolation and boredom and not primarily lack of accommodation. Most social services departments in the sample had arrangements with housing departments to make local authority accommodation available to young people in care, often meaning that young people in care have an advantage over their peers. It must be added that most of this accommodation is some of the poorest available from the local authority. In Sunderland and Bradford, for example, young people in care were frequently able to obtain accommodation on leaving care but, given the shortage of available accommodation and priority given to homeless families, it was primarily 'hard to let' council property on the outer estates.

40. Heads of community homes reported a complex of factors occurring; young people leaving care are nervous and unsure in any case, unemployment removes a source of security and stability to help them through this. Depression can set in, self-discipline suffers and budgeting is prejudiced. Being alone and lacking money develops the attractiveness of crime and drugs. We found the following evidence from the sample authorities.

41. *Financial Impact* — *Low incomes make independent living difficult for all people, but young people formerly in care tend to have* *low skills in money management and self-care, particularly if they have been in residential care for a long time.* For example, Harrow reported an increase in the number of young people who were formerly in care having difficulty paying their rent. Liberal use of supplementation and section 27 payments by the social services department have helped. Officers in charge find that the employment situation directly affects the final phase of preparation for independence. This is because of the economics of living independently in a flat on £25 per week; even taking into account grants and rent rebates, young inexperienced and worldly immature people find it very difficult to face this future.

42. In Lambeth debts to bodies such as LEB, the rent boards and HP catalogue companies are on the increase amongst young people who have left care. Borrowing amongst friends and relatives puts stress on personal relationships. The lack of income means that young people live from one cheque to another with insufficient money to meet heating and lighting bills or to furnish their flats. The young people in the Bradford After Care Group said that living on supplementary benefit makes it almost impossible to survive in a flat. Those who could not get a council flat often could not afford a privately rented flat as they did not have the necessary deposit. Many young people could not cope on benefits and returned to the department for support, particularly with debt problems.

43. ***Social Impact of Unemployment on Children Leaving Care*** — The problems facing unemployed young people trying to live independently after leaving care tend to be boredom and isolation resulting from lack of social contact. *Young people find it difficult enough to cope on their own when leaving care but where unemployment means nothing to do, boredom and the removal of one vital source of contacts this exacerbates the situation.* People frequently make their adult friends in the workplace and removal of work is a loss of the main source of social contact for most people. Young people who have been in care are in particular need of social contacts.

44. In particular contact with adults, of which young people in care are particularly deprived, has been of great value and is unlikely to be available anywhere other than in the workplace. *Unemployment has severely deprived young people of these valuable contacts, which other young people find in their family or adult friends of parents.*

> 'Young people who are unemployed are deprived of adult contact in work situations which hitherto would have helped them learn more about the "adult" world. This is of particular importance for young people who have been in care as they require the maximum assistance to successfully integrate into the wider community. As they often lack family support, relationships with older colleagues in a work environment would provide substitute care, advice and assistance. Without these relationships, those leaving care are more isolated and dependent on their contemporaries and their own resources.' (Officer in charge of home, Bradford)

Similar experiences were reported by other authorities and in some a need for social work support or day care facilities to help young people establish themselves was recognised.

45. In Sunderland and Bradford many young people leaving care move into flats on the large outlying estates. Although such accommodation is readily available to young people leaving care it is often of very poor quality and the environment is far from ideal. Jobs are much less numerous on the estates than in other areas, and to find any work the young people have to travel into the centre of town. Those living on supplementary benefit find it difficult to finance travel over longer distances. The oppressive, unfriendly atmosphere of the estates highlights the feelings of loneliness, isolation and despair young people leaving care already experience.

46. ***Social Work Support in the Community*** — *In response to the difficulties young people who have left care are having in surviving independently, there was some evidence that authorities are increasing social work support in the community for children who have left care.* This has started from a very low base as previously authorities have not seen it as a major part of their responsibilities. The support offered comes from either residential social workers, field social workers or specialist social workers. Residential workers are increasingly likely to maintain contact with young people who have left care. For example, in Sunderland staff in a specialist unit working with young people approaching their departure from care, maintain a gradually decreasing contact with the young people once they leave the unit. In Bradford two after-care workers have been appointed specifically to help young people who have left care. They also run an after-care group for young people. We spoke to young people in this group; all were unemployed and felt the after-care group filled a real need. Each faced problems coping after leaving care, in particular isolation and loneliness after being in community homes where they were rarely alone. They felt that loneliness and isolation would not be such a problem if they were employed and could meet more people.

Conclusion

47. The evidence from the survey revealed an extremely worrying level of unemployment amongst children in care, far in excess of that in the 16 to 18 age population as a whole. Many community homes in those areas with highest unemployment have 100% of their young people out of work. At best less than half of residents of working age in community homes are unable to find work. The results of this disturbing prevalence of unemployment are that insecure, unstable and disadvantaged young people are suffering a further disadvantage. Staff of homes are under increasing pressure. Young people are finding it decreasingly possible to survive on their own in the urban environment on leaving care. These compound into increased likelihood of crime, drug taking and other anti-social behaviour.

48. Unemployment begins to influence young people in care even before they leave school when faced with the certainty of being unemployed. As a result non-school attendance and delinquency are more likely. Young people in community homes in the sample authorities now seem very unlikely to find work. This puts pressure on staff who now have to maintain cover during the day and try to keep young people occupied and using their time usefully. Staff are also involved more in helping young people find work or to sign on and claim benefit. The prolonged boredom and frustration of unemployment add to the pressure young people in care already feel and can lead to unpredictable or delinquent behaviour. The full scenario is summed up by the following comments by an officer in charge of a community home in Lambeth:

> 'Children/young people from the age of 12 upwards are no longer swallowing the old tales of "be good, attend school, get a good report, get qualifications and therefore a good career." Unemployment can have the effect of taking away hope, self-respect etc and nurtures boredom. The outcome of unemployment has caused increases in the already difficult problem of managing bored, hopeless young

people in increasing numbers during the day. (They often want to lie in bed in the morning and stop out at night.) Outcome is increasing staffing requirement day and night.'

49. The impression from social workers and heads of homes is that the in-care population is ageing and that older teenagers are more likely to come into care than in the past. There was evidence that young people are remaining in community and foster homes to older ages than previously.

50. Children leaving care find it more difficult to survive independently if unemployed; the financial difficulties of surviving on their own on supplementary benefit with little experience of budgeting are severe. Coupled to this the social impact of loneliness and boredom are a further burden as is the loss of valuable contact with adults which would have been gained in the workplace. There is a clear need, as identified by the House of Commons Social Services Committee,[11] for continued support by social services departments for children once they have left care.

51. There was no direct evidence of a link between unemployment and crime amongst young people, although there was a strong impression amongst social workers and heads of homes that unemployment created both the opportunity and pressures which are more likely to lead to crime.

52. Residential social workers in the areas with the most serious unemployment now find that it is impossible to use employment as a realistic target for young people in care. There was much evidence of this in Bradford, Knowsley and Sunderland. This has an impact on preparing young people for leaving care and giving them an aim in life and a reason to exert self-discipline. A head of home in Bradford reported that as employment does not now feature in targets set for individuals, the aim is simply to get young people to use their time as constructively as possible.

Chapter 4
Unemployment and Mental Illness

Recent Research

1. The relationship between work and health is one of great complexity. Both physical and mental well-being may be promoted by satisfying work in acceptable conditions and may equally be caused to deteriorate where work is monotonous, frustrating, hazardous, inadequately compensated or carried out in unsuitable surroundings. For an individual, therefore, unemployment may arguably come as a tremendous blow or as a blessing in disguise.

2. Recently research has attempted to establish unemployment as an independent cause of mental and physical suffering. Generally speaking the experience of unemployment has been found to yield few of the imputed benefits of freedom and extended leisure. Unemployed people are largely poor, restricted by money worries and debts and unable to participate effectively in everyday social life let alone in creative outside activities. Indeed all evidence suggests that unemployed people retreat and withdraw from society the longer their unemployment continues. They also tend to become less healthy in body and mind than their contemporaries at work and are likely to die earlier through disease, accident or suicide.

3. Following Jahoda's pioneering studies in the 1930s,[1] numerous aspects of the connection between unemployment and physical ill health have been examined, including surveys among unemployed workers, prospective studies, macrostatistical studies and individual case histories.[2] Of special interest in the UK has been an MSC study which found that of the long-term unemployed, 37% said they had a handicap or an illness and 13% were registered disabled.[3] Elsewhere macrostatistical studies such as Brenner's have asserted an association between cycles of boom and slump and changes in mortality rates, suicide, heart attacks and so forth.[4] Most recently a major study conducted at the City University has confirmed that unemployment leads to premature death for men and makes their wives more vulnerable too.[5] This study was based on findings of the 1971 Census when only 4% of the work-force was unemployed and so raises questions about the effects of unemployment on health at the current unemployment rate of over 13%.

4. Peter Warr's studies at Sheffield have gone a long way towards confirming the mental ill health that can result from unemployment.[6] Warr has taken scales of high and low well-being, the latter characterised by anxiety, depression, low morale, lack of self-confidence, low sense of personal autonomy, inability to cope with the problems of living and dissatisfaction with oneself and the social and physical environment. His results suggest very strongly that the transition to unemployment yields a marked reduction in well-being and regaining a job restores it. Daniel has also shown that the degree of stress tends to vary according to the importance of a person's job as a focus of personal identity.[7] Fagin's family studies confirm this and also show how unemployment may affect the health of other family members besides that of the unemployed themselves. Both wives and the children of unemployed male breadwinners were found to exhibit symptoms of depression, despair and apathy.[8]

5. Suicide is one aspect of mental depression that appears to occur more frequently among the unemployed. During the 1930s the suicide rate in the UK peaked for both men and women at 6,000 a year. A steady decline in suicide after the war was brought to a halt in the mid 1970s by, it would seem, the renewed onset of unemployment, with suicides reaching over 4,000 in 1978 as unemployment rose to 1.5 million. Between 1979 and 1980 the numbers increased again by 2.9% to a total of 4,300 suicides in 1980.[9] Analysis of the OPCS figures from 1971-1981 shows suicide rates for unemployed men of twice the national average, together with much higher rates of accidental death and fatal disease. The overall death rate was 36% higher than normal and amongst the wives of the unemployed the death rates were also 20% higher.[10] In Edinburgh Platt has found a strong association between unemployment, suicide and attempted suicide (parasuicide) and has also established that parasuicide rates tend to increase with lengthening durations of unemployment. In 1982, those unemployed for less than six months had a relative risk of parasuicide of 6.2%; this rose to 10.4% among those unemployed for between six and twelve months and to 18.9% among those unemployed for over twelve months.[11]

6. Although middle-aged male breadwinners are particularly vulnerable to mental illness after sudden unemployment,[12] there is substantial evidence to suggest that the young are also at risk. According to a study based on interviews with over 1,000 young people who had visited the London Central YMCA, one in four of unemployed 16-25 year olds may have contemplated suicide. Whilst 17% of young people with no experience of unemployment may consider suicide, this figure jumps to 24% among the short-term unemployed and 26% among the long-term.[13] Such findings can be linked to other research on young people which has shown how the destruction of self-image that accompanies unemployment has moved down the years to the young.[14]

7. In the AMA's research, interest has been focused on the links between unemployment and mental ill health, not forgetting that the borderline between physical and mental sickness is often blurred. With the NHS, the social services are responsible for the welfare of mentally ill people, a role which has been increasing in importance as dehospitalisation policies have taken hold. It follows that any increase in the range or degree of mental illness within the population is likely to make itself felt in local authority workloads. The evidence that mental illness appears to become more prevalent as a result of unemployment suggests that services may become overstretched or prove inadequate as unemployment rises. Accordingly, part of the AMA survey has concentrated on the effect of unemployment on services for mentally ill people. Figures have been collected where possible on both hospital admissions and referrals to local authorities for community support of various kinds. An attempt has also been made to build up a picture of employ-

ment status at the time a client comes into contact with the local authority and of his or her employment prospects on returning to the community. Throughout it has been noted that current difficulties are being compounded by community care policies, encouraging the release of patients from mental hospitals into communities lacking the resources to care for them and where their employment prospects are minimal.[15,16]

Findings from the Survey

Psychiatric Patients and Mental Health Referrals

8. Initially information was sought on the numbers of psychiatric patients being admitted to hospital on an in-patient or day-care basis, numbers being referred to social services departments and numbers in group homes, sheltered accommodation, hostels and day centres. Information was patchy and incomplete, suggesting few regular lines of communication between local health authorities and social services departments and maybe also a lack of knowledge of what is happening to the mentally ill in different areas.

9. No general pattern emerged from this investigation, although dehospitalisation policies are clearly widespread and increasingly compulsory admissions are giving way to more informal types of treatment. In Coventry, for example, numbers treated as in-patients showed little change between 1978/9 and 1982/3, except for a sudden rise in 1981 when incidentally unemployment also accelerated. The numbers of day-care patients actually fell, as shown in Table 1.

Table 1 — Number of Admissions to Psychiatric Hospitals in Coventry

	1978/79	1979/80	1980/81	1981/82	1982/83
In-patient	1,683	1,693	1,943	1,804	1,688
Day-care	8,849	7,933	8,272	8,042	7,205

10. In Sunderland in-patient numbers rose by about 20% but again day-care admissions fell.

Table 2 — Number of Admissions to Psychiatric Hospitals in Sunderland

	1978/79	1979/80	1980/81	1981/82	1982/83	
In-patient	998	1,129	1,161	1,070	1,242	
Day-care	5,976	5,823	7,525	7,994	8,794	Day Hospital
Day-care	6,283	4,408	3,506	1,998	2,140	Main Hospital
Total Day-care	12,259	10,231	11,031	9,992	10,934	

Likewise in Tower Hamlets out-patient attendances for psychiatric patients fell:

Table 3 — Out-patient Attendances for Psychiatric Patients in Tower Hamlets

Year	New Patients	Total Patients
1978	1,398	16,078
1979	1,331	16,860
1980	1,268	14,227
1981	1,213	16,405
1982	1,122	14,822
1983	1,313	15,195

11. In Knowsley, figures for the Mersey Regional Health Authority show total admissions up from 10,200 in 1979 to 11,300 in 1981, with informal admissions rising from 9,400 in 1979 to 10,600 by 1981 and subsequent admissions from 7,050 in 1979 to 8,200 in 1981. Within these the admission rate for Knowsley itself is estimated to have increased from 2.8 per 1,000 population to 3.1 per 1,000. In Harrow the number of admissions to psychiatric hospitals also rose: 1978/9 - 598, 1979/80 - 442, 1980/81 - 549, 1981/82-634, 1982/83-866.

12. It is a truism that the provision of beds and treatment and the numbers of patients admitted to any hospital is not necessarily a reflection of the degree of ill health of a population. In the case of mental illness this would seem to be a particularly pertinent observation. If, that is, one accepts the previously cited research on the link between rising unemployment and increasing mental ill health, one cannot interpret these figures to mean that mental health is improving in Coventry, Sunderland and Tower Hamlets and at the same time deteriorating in Knowsley and Harrow. Rather these figures indicate local health authority policies and resources.

13. Arguably a more consistent picture of the mental health of a local population may be deduced from the increasing or decreasing numbers of mental health problems referred to social services departments. In the three authorities where figures could be obtained, an increase in such referrals was clear, and moreover in line with the area's relative unemployment rates, i.e. in 1983 Harrow had an unemployment rate of approximately 6%, Coventry approximately 15%, and Sunderland approximately 17%.

Table 4 — Total Number of Mental Health Referrals

	1978/79	1979/80	1980/81	1981/82	1982/83	1983/84
Harrow	—	285	289	321	321	—
Sunderland	180	187	367	580	679	904
(referrals where mental health was the primary problem)						
Coventry	757	996	871	976	1,044	—

This seems to offer a tentative confirmation that in the present economic climate mental health problems are on the increase and are increasingly impingeing on the social services.

14. Information was also requested on the numbers of the mentally ill in group homes, sheltered accommodation, hostels and day centres. Only in Manchester, where provision is extensive, and in Harrow had day-centre places been increased. Elsewhere provision had remained static or had fallen. Sunderland noted that one of its two hostels for the mentally ill had been closed in 1982. Tower Hamlets, having built a new hostel, leased it to the local health authority for five years as they could not afford to staff or run it. Generally speaking, therefore, local authority provision for the mentally ill is far from adequate if it is accepted that mental illness is an increasingly troublesome aspect of life in the 1980s. As a result increasing reliance is being placed on voluntary services such as those provided by MIND, the Richmond Fellowship, the Salvation Army and so forth.

Employment Prospects and Mentally Ill People

15. Authorities were asked if they were planning any new initiatives for the mentally ill directly related to unemployment. Answers were mostly negative, mainly because of the impossibility of finding work. For this and other therapeutic reasons counselling and the development of social skills were seen as more important. The few job-creation initiatives that were encountered do suggest that much more could be achieved in this direction were the impetus there. In Harrow for example the development of a group packaging activity had proved both successful, satisfying and self-supporting and in Tower Hamlets lithography had been introduced and it was thought that photography could also be started at a relatively low cost if the funds were forthcoming.

16. Arrangements with local employers for finding work for the mentally ill were also more or less non-existent, though clearly there had been some in the past. In Sunderland mentally ill people had previously been found work in laundries or refuse collection. In Harrow links had existed with major local firms. Links with the Disablement Resettlement Officer, as indeed in all authorities, had also been helpful. However, these sources of employment have gradually dried up during the past two to three years and there are now no openings available in Harrow for the employment of mentally ill people. Even the DRO has been unable to place applicants in employment with other local firms. In other authorities links with the DRO also seem to be weaker than in the past. In Sunderland it was said that the numbers being referred to the DRO were decreasing, mainly because clients were actually refusing to go to the DRO for fear of being put on rehabilitation courses, declared fit for employment and then subsequently unemployed. This then would result in their benefit levels being reduced.

17. Amongst local employers a sad lack of concern seems to be forthcoming. People are not very interested in helping the mentally ill back to health. In Knowsley, for example, we were told of discussions between local employers, GPs, and clergy and other community leaders to discuss making employment available for the mentally ill. Only one person turned up. Mentally ill people at a time of high unemployment are therefore in a very difficult situation as far as rehabilitation is concerned. Ann Birch has illustrated these problems in her recent study of the mentally ill in Manchester for MIND, 'What Chance Have We Got?', showing how common it is after discharge from hospital for the recovering patients to be dragged down into depression again by unemployment with its consequent boredom and low income.[17] Moreover the stigma of mental illness was found to deter people from seeking out other activities in, for example, adult education.

18. Because it has become more difficult to find employment for those who have been, or those who are, mentally ill, those in local authority homes, centres and hostels are tending to stay on longer. In Coventry the length of stay of clients in centres and hostels has been noticeably affected, particularly for younger persons and for males. Figures from Harrow provided the most exact statement of the problem:

Table 5 — Clients Discharged from Day Centre to New Jobs in Open Employment in Harrow

1973	14 clients, average stay 10 weeks
1981	10 clients, average stay 16 weeks
1982	10 clients, average stay 17½ weeks
1983	7 clients, average stay 28½ weeks
1984	None to date.

Thus greater numbers of clients are now in fact faced with fewer facilities due to the inability of individuals to move back to work.

Changes in Policies for Supporting Mentally Ill People

19. Moving back into full employment after recovering from a mental illness is not of course the only nor necessarily the ideal course of action for many people. Surveying the whole discussion, Hayes and Nutman have suggested that there are three factors in the situation that need to be considered as changeable: firstly, the clients themselves and the treatment they receive; secondly, the organisations within which people work and the hierarchies of responsibility involved as well as the patterns of work and time; thirdly, the nature of work itself and of attitudes to those gainfully employed and those involved in other activities, such as voluntary work and housework.[18] Social services can do little about the second and third factors, which are out of their control, but they do have scope for action within the first category and some have already started to meet the challenge.

20. One popular development to meet increased need has been the growth of the 'drop-in' centre. This has resulted partly from the realisation that traditional day centres meet only one segment of need and may not be appropriate for some people, as is suggested by their moderate success with regard to rehabilitation. For many in such centres, basic packaging work and a few poorly supported extra activities may provide the only occupations. Clients regard attending such centres as 'going to work' and little effort may then be made to assist people back into the real world of work. This is not true of well run day centres where the value of therapy and creative activity is understood, but it is true of some.

21. New policy is being developed around the belief that the mentally ill should become part of a social network with regular contacts, with entrance to work a secondary target. As is frequently found, idealism is closely backed by economics! In Lambeth a move from a hospital-based day centre to a drop-in centre immediately saved £25,000 previously paid to the health authority. Other similar drop-in centres are often funded by voluntary bodies, usually with the support of local authority grants. In Manchester and Coventry, MIND has drop-in centres. In Manchester a unit for young mentally ill people known as '42nd Street', a suitably attractive and unrevealing title, has proved successful but is experiencing pressure from rising costs and demand for places. In Coventry the centre has a 25 regular clients daily, a number built up since its opening only 18 months ago.

22. The Lambeth drop-in centre has proved so acceptable that even with a limited catchment area it is experiencing pressure from heavy demand. The growth of clients is judged to be partly a result of hospital discharge policy (about one third of clients are long-stay hospital patients recently discharged), and partly a result of the attendance of difficult clients like alcoholics and drug addicts whom others reject. The real growth area, however, is seen to be amongst the under-30s and especially amongst young blacks who are coming to the centre in increasing numbers. These young people often have quite severe emotional problems and this is affecting an increasingly younger age group. Most are unemployed and most in fact have never worked at all. *This growth of younger, mentally ill clients was extensively remarked upon.* In Knowsley such youngsters were expected to stay unemployed indefinitely and in fact to remain 'a problem to the social services for the rest of their lives'. Amongst the Knowsley clients it is the 20-24 year-olds who have grown in number most noticeably. They are bored, feel they are not needed and lack a sense of self-worth intimately related to their being unemployed. The thing that such young people still want most is a job.

23. Older individuals are also felt to have grown in numbers, though no proof could be given of this. In Coventry, where experience of sudden, first-time redundancy has been particularly widespread, the middle-aged with no previous unemployment background were felt to be especially at risk of mental illness, in fact more so than young people. In Bradford, similar to Coventry in its recent experience of unemployment, this was thought to be particularly a problem for Asian parents and was illustrated by reference to suicide figures.

24. In Bradford there were 1,200 attempted suicides in 1983. Unemployment was seen as a major cause with very few attempted suicides made by those in full employment. Attempted suicide has increased most notably amongst Asian women where unemployment amongst husbands is seen as the major cause. The Asian financial structure is very different from that of the white communities as Asians are expected to contribute to the community and extended families. Consequently, unemployment and loss of income affects more people and creates a feeling of failure and of letting the community down. Mental illness resulting from this is seen as a punishment from God and is very difficult to acknowledge as a problem publicly. Generally it is felt in Bradford that the caring agencies see only the 'tip of the iceberg' and there is no way of knowing the true impact of unemployment as a contributory factor in mental health problems.

25. In most authorities education is also seen as holding out new hope to the mentally ill for rebuilding confidence, self-image and acquiring marketable skills. In Knowsley talks have been on-going with Kirkby College in the hopes of working out useful programmes and in Harrow courses are already being taken up by clients at Hatch End College. As with the mentally and physically handicapped the nature of the relationship between the key officers in the social services and in the further education colleges seems to be a crucial factor in the achievement of courses of suitable content and length.

26. Finally in some authorities use of voluntary services, such as 'meals on wheels', as something to which the unemployed mentally ill may contribute has worked very well. This is a different dimension from the world of work but one in which an identity is important and reliability and competence matter a great deal. In Harrow it has been found that some mentally ill patients in the course of recovery have both benefited from and contributed effectively to such activities. This is surely a course of action worth pursuing.

Conclusion

27. During interviews, some officers suggested that unemployment might indeed be crucial in either unbalancing individuals or rehabilitating mentally ill people. To a schizophrenic or seriously disturbed individual, however, a high level of unemployment would make little difference. In other words, sick people would be sick whatever their environment. Many psychologists would argue, however, that no mental illness, whatever its genetic origins, can be properly understood outside its social context. Anthony Storr has recently commented that

> 'Patients do better in societies in which they are cared for principally at home, in which work can be adjusted to their capabilities, and in which being labelled "schizophrenic" (for example) does not produce stigma. Since work is a valuable preventer of relapse, we may expect that, in times of high unemployment, the outlook for schizophrenics becomes worse.'[19]

If this is true, most mentally ill individuals of working age will be affected by high levels of unemployment to some degree.

28. The evidence from this survey shows, however, that local authority social services are in no position to cope with increasing demands from mentally ill people. In most cases conventional provision of places in group homes, in sheltered accommodation, in hostels and in day centres has remained static or has fallen. At the same time open employment opportunities have almost disappeared so that those in day centres are remaining in them for longer, with diminishing chances of proper rehabilitation. An increase in younger, mentally ill clients is also creating urgent new demands which, at current levels of provision, cannot be adequately met.

New policies, for drop-in centres, for further education and for community work, are meeting with some success, but at the moment they are too limited in scope to make a real contribution to the needs of mentally ill people at a time of high unemployment.

Chapter 5
Unemployment and Financial Hardship

Review of Literature and Research

1. There is much that is unknown or unproven about the social and economic effects of unemployment. However, what is both clear and well documented is that the majority of people who become unemployed suffer a fall in income. To go further: 'The only things that we seem to know about the unemployed with complete certainty are that they have no jobs and they are mostly very poor. . . .'[1]

2. Most unemployed people live on supplementary benefit, which in 1983/4 was £59.20 for a married couple with two children plus a housing benefit top-up to cover rent. In 1983 the Family Expenditure Survey estimated that on average households spend £125.79 a week (excluding housing).[2] Therefore the unemployed family has to live on 40% less than that required by the average family; 41% of all unemployed people are totally dependent on supplementary benefit. The level of social security support for the unemployed is a matter of political dispute involving such issues as work incentives. However, Bradshaw, Cooke and Godfrey[3] argue cogently that the supplementary benefit rate was not designed to cope either with large-scale or long-term unemployment and graphically demonstrate the consequences of this. Living standards of the unemployed are shown to be worse than those of the low paid. Bradshaw et al demonstrate that the long-term unemployed are living on just over half (57%) of the gross income of the long-term employed. The consequences of this poverty are numerous, many of which are likely to have an effect on the number and type of social services clients. One such area which is both most widely researched and the focus of this study, is financial hardship and debt.

3. Evidence which will be presented later suggests that social services departments are dealing with increasing numbers of people with severe debt problems or in need of help with social security benefits. Local authorities have a limited statutory responsibility to react to these growing enquiries in their duty to prevent children coming into care under Section 1 of the 1980 Child Care Act.

4. Research findings confirm that unemployment is creating increased financial hardship and debt, or that this is one of the major pathologies of unemployment. Daniel[4] has demonstrated that 72% of a group concerned at being out of work reported worries about money, whilst 58% mentioned social or psychological costs (see Table 1). Daniel also identifies that in his sample of 1,479 unemployed people, 16% of those having financial difficulties mentioned problems over gas/electricity/heating bills, and 13% cited problems over paying rent or mortgage;

Table 1 — Reason for Being Concerned about Unemployment

	Total %
Lack of money	72
Boredom/inactivity	28
Depression/apathy	14
Feel failure/useless	11
Social isolation	4
Social rejection	1
Others	1
Don't know	1
Total	132

(Totals add to more than 100 per cent because some respondents gave more that one reason.)

Source: Daniel, W. W. **A National Survey of the Unemployed**, PEP, 1974.

5. A joint working party report by the Welsh Office and Directors of Social Services[5] commented on Daniel's findings as follows:

> 'What does emerge from this data is. . . that the financial problems of the unemployed are very much the kind of problems which already consume the efforts of social work staff, regardless of the original reason for their involvement. Indeed it seems reasonable to suppose that the additional financial problems brought about by unemployment are likely to result firstly in referrals being made to social services departments which would otherwise not have been made, secondly in social work intervention being more intensive than it otherwise would have been, and thirdly in that intervention lasting longer than it otherwise might have done'.

6. Other studies have arrived at the same sorts of conclusions on the basis of an impressive body of evidence. Research has focused on most parts of Great Britain, although primarily on areas of high unemployment. In a major survey of unemployed people in the east side of Newcastle, Newcastle City Council[6] report that increasing unemployment is causing severe financial problems for greater numbers of families. High incidence of indebtedness and significant difficulties meeting essential financial commitments, especially amongst households with a long-term unemployed head, emerged from the survey. The growth of these financial problems was found to be having a major effect on the work of the social services department. The main findings included:

(i) A marked growth in referrals to area offices for financial problems; particularly noticeable were fuel debt referrals, running at almost twice their 1979 levels.

(ii) A noticeable increase in new cases at the Walker Welfare Rights Service where the service is no longer publicised and occasionally closed in order to contain demand within a manageable level.

(iii) Reporting by a number of voluntary agencies of an increase in requests for financial advice and information and for financial assistance from financial trusts.

(iv) Financial problem referrals form a significant proportion of all referrals; fuel debt problems alone now account for around 10% of referrals.

(v) The long-term unemployed in particular made significant use of the social services department and other agencies for advice and information, usually on financial matters. Over one third of households with long-term unemployed heads and a quarter of households with short-term unemployed heads had had contact with either area offices of the department, the Welfare Rights Service, the Walker Resource Centre or Byker CDP in the last year alone.

7. Some figures give the background to these conclusions: 42% of households with an unemployed head experienced difficulty with paying rent compared with 23% in other households. Serious rent arrears were greater amongst households with unemployed heads. 46% of households with unemployed heads reported difficulty with paying heating bills compared with 18% of households containing no unemployed people. 20% of the unemployed households said they had been unable to pay a bill in the last year compared with 2% of households with an employed head. This led Newcastle Social Services Department to conclude:

> 'Because increasing unemployment lies behind these changes a significant proportion of the people with these difficulties may never have faced financial problems of this kind before. The experience of recurrent or persistent financial problems may in some circumstances generate the need for more intensive, long-term social work intervention. Appropriate handling of financial problem referrals may forestall in certain cases the need for intensive social work intervention.'

8. Strathclyde Regional Social Work Department[7] report similar findings in their area:

> 'Two recent studies within Strathclyde are highlighting quite dramatically the complex social and financial problems that arise from long-term unemployment.'

Social work teams in Strathclyde reported an increasing number of people with financial difficulties amongst their workloads and also an increase in the numbers of people with rent arrears. In the Clydebank area where unemployment rose by 27% in one year as a result of the closure of a large plant, casework with families rose by 23% and rent arrears increased by 21%.

9. Sheffield City Council[8] looked at change in six social work referral categories over the period July 1976 to June 1981 one of which was 'help/advice, financial or material'. This analysis uncovered the following patterns in referrals in these categories:-

Table 2 — Financial Referrals — Sheffield

Year	Average No. of Referrals Per Month
Help/Advice Financial or Material	
1976 (July–Dec)	185.3
1977	230.1
1978 (January–October)	212
1979 (March–December)	202.3
1980	247.3
1981 (to June)	268.5

10. Financial difficulties are not only being experienced by those formerly receiving low pay, as a recent report by the Money Advice Development Project in the West Midlands illustrates:

> 'It is no longer just the poor who cannot manage; wide spread redundancy has created a new class of debtors — the white collar or skilled worker. . . — unemployment can throw into confusion families that have always handled their household bills perfectly competently in the past.'[9]

The majority of the problems dealt with by the West Midlands project workers involved essentials such as rent, rates, fuel and clothing.

A study of referrals to a social work team by Nash[10] demonstrated that unemployed people and their families were not primarily seeking help with the emotional problems but mainly with practical and financial requirements: 'Many were indicative of a chronic and worsening situation and a gradual deterioration in living standards and personal relationships'.

11. The general impact of financial hardship amongst unemployed families in terms of stress, turmoil and family breakdown is largely undocumented. The Newcastle survey however indicated that there was some evidence of a likely long-term impact on the need for social work interventions. The report however identifies a more specific and easily measurable impact in terms of requests for help with financial hardship and debt and help with welfare rights advice. Research in Sheffield, Newcastle and elsewhere demonstrates an increase in the number of such enquiries to social services departments during recent years. This need has become sufficiently intense and specific in some areas that specialist officers have been appointed. For example, Gateshead Metropolitan Borough appointed a Welfare Rights Financial Adviser specialising in advice on debt in May 1983. The reasons for creating the post were:

> 'The post was established in response to the rising level of unemployment, the declining value of state benefits and the fall in the general purchasing power of wages which were producing an increasing incidence of debt related problems.' (Report to Gateshead Social Services Committee)

Findings from Survey

12. ***Definitions*** — This section covers all areas of work by social services departments (SSDs), or local authorities, concerned with advice or assistance of a monetary nature. This includes: first, 'welfare rights' — advice and assistance with social security benefits; second, debts, including fuel debts, unpaid bills, rent and rate arrears; and third, general inability to meet outgoing expenses. Any of these can comprise a 'financial referral' to a social worker. Financial help by social services departments includes payments under Section 1 of the Child Care Act 1980 and applications to charities to meet specific and urgent financial and material needs.

13. ***The Trend in Referrals*** — The questionnaire sought numerical information to establish the trend in social work cases manifesting primarily a financial problem. This exercise was made difficult because of different administrative arrangements in the sample authorities and incomplete or non-existent records. 'Welfare rights', for example, is frequently a recent addition to referral recording categories.

In most of the authorities in the sample welfare rights and financial advice was offered by all field social workers. However the predominant modes of providing this service in each of the sample authorities were as follows:-

(i) A separate Welfare Rights Service within the social services department; as in Manchester, Knowsley.

(ii) All social workers deal with welfare rights; as in Tower Hamlets and Harrow.

(iii) A voluntary organisation e.g. Citizen Advice Bureau runs a Welfare Rights Service on an agency basis for the local authority as in Coventry.

(iv) Welfare Rights/Advisory Service run elsewhere in the council other than the social services department; as in Sunderland, Bradford and Lambeth.

Whatever administrative arrangements were in operation in the sample, an increase in welfare rights activity has cost implications for the local authority, and in most cases this relates to the social services budget.

Financial Referrals to Social Workers

14. Under this heading the aim was to collect numerical data derived from social services department's records of social work referrals which contained a category where financial difficulty (including welfare rights if not separately recorded) was the major presenting problem of the case concerned. Of those authorities maintaining such records the following results were obtained:-

Table 3 — Number of New Financial Referrals to Social Services Departments

Authority	Year				% Change 1979/80–1982/83
	1979/80	1980/81	1981/82	1982/83	
Sunderland	250	292	362	502	+101%
Tower Hamlets	469	587	578	709	+51%
Harrow	333	436	479	446	+34%
Coventry	4,527	3,899	4,937	5,319	+17.5%

15. *The welter of financial referrals demonstrates a significantly increasing trend in this category of referrals over the past five years — the period of greatest increase in unemployment.* Qualitative information supports this. *All authorities in the sample report that social workers have been dealing with an increasing proportion and number of cases where the major (or a main) problem is of a financial nature.* However, not all are able to offer numerical evidence of this. The pattern varies according to the administrative arrangements for welfare rights/financial referrals mentioned above.

16. Interviews with social workers and team leaders in the whole sample revealed a clear trend of increasing incidence and intensity of financial referrals in the last five or six years. *The view of field workers in the sample authorities was that financial and welfare rights referrals are the most significant and easily identifiable impact of unemployment on their case loads.* This directly results from the difficulty people living on supplementary benefit have in coping financially. Not only is it a question of financial difficulty alone but financial stress in turn has led to an increase in marital stress and breakdown. An area team in Sunderland reported that in the last year only about three or four marital dispute cases did not involve people in receipt of supplementary benefit.

17. Financial difficulties are not always the single factor in a referral and are often linked to another problem such as marital dispute. One social work team in Sunderland reported a significant increase in family referrals with a preventative input since 1975. They describe these referrals as complex involving a number of problems: including relationships, fuel bills and finance. The first layer of difficulty in such cases is usually financial and social workers concentrate first on dealing with this, i.e. clearing bills, settling benefit entitlement, and delaying fuel disconnections. Often, once the financial difficulties are put in some sort of order, the relationship problems begin to resolve themselves as the way forward looks clearer. In some cases, financial problems mask other fundamental difficulties. Such scenarios are increasing and involve a lot of social work time, i.e. first isolating the difficulties then negotiating with fuel boards, housing departments and other agencies.

18. There were conflicting views from social workers and advice workers concerning the attitude of unemployed people towards debt. In one area team they report that unemployed people have a non-caring attitude to debt because there is no final sanction against their indebtedness: 'the most a court can take from you is £1 per week.' In another authority a Citizens Advice Bureau (CAB) debt counsellor said that on the contrary unemployed people were very concerned with debts; the problem was that in their haste they tend to pay the first person who comes calling at the door, and fail to pay the crucial creditors who can cut off their fuel supply, for example.

19. On the whole creditors tend to be more sympathetic with unemployed than with newly employed people. *This however does not last forever and in fact the longer one is unemployed, the worse debt* *problems are likely to become.* This is because, firstly, creditors can be kept in abeyance for the first six months or so, but are then unable to help further. Secondly, people are often helped during the first six months to a year of unemployment by redundancy pay and full unemployment benefit.

20. Coventry Social Services Department and CAB report particularly acute debt problems locally, the cause being the sudden arrival of unemployment and the former high average wages. Coventry had a predominance of 'affluent workers', large numbers of whom are now unemployed following the decline of such industries as motor car manufacturing; many took on mortgages and credit on the strength of their high wages but are now faced with severe debts.

21. The trend in fuel disconnections is variable and depends on fuel board and DHSS practices locally. However, there is some evidence of increases particularly in the north. Other similar, but more recent, debt problems were reported by social workers in various authorities; amongst these were a growth in water disconnections and furniture removed by hire purchase companies. With these, as with fuel debts, people come to the social services department for help.

Section 1 Payments (Child Care Act 1980)

22. Social services departments have special power under section 1 of the Child Care Act 1980 to make financial payments which are aimed 'to prevent children coming into care'. 'Section 1' payments are made in the expectation that the solving of the presenting financial difficulty will solve or reduce other problems which may cause children to come into care.

23. Numerical data on local expenditure on 'section 1' was obtained from the sample authorities and the questionnaire yielded fairly comprehensive information. However, with the exception of Sunderland, the increase in expenditure on, or payments under 'section 1', between 1978/9 and 1982/3 were either at or below the rate of inflation. In Sunderland however there was a 152.7% increase in section 1 payments over this period.

Tower Hamlets were also able to identify an increase in 'section 1' specifically for financial hardship. Much of this is concentrated in the dockland area of the borough where deprivation and unemployment are highest.

24. Interviews with officers of social services departments led to the conclusion that 'section 1' expenditure is not a good indicator of increased need arising from financial hardship. In budget making the 'section 1' heading is more easily constrained than others, being a discrete financial heading, monitored and controlled through strict financial limits when necessary. 'Section 1' therefore reflects policies and practice more than need.

Welfare Rights

25. This is probably the most direct indicator of change in service demand resulting from unemployment as the majority of unemployed people are dependent on social security benefits. Numbers of people solely dependent on supplementary benefit and other means-tested benefits have increased with unemployment.

26. The questionnaire firstly asked for numerical data on welfare rights referrals to social services departments. This covers both referrals to specialist Welfare Rights Officers and to social workers in general:-

Table 4 — Welfare Rights Referrals

	YEAR					
Authority	**1978/79**	**1979/80**	**1980/81**	**1981/82**	**1982/83**	**% Change 1978/79–1982/83**
Harrow	6,369	7,214	7,849	8,002	8,501	+31%
Knowsley	Only available for one area — no increase					
Coventry	1,857	1,969	1,745	2,221	2,712	+46%
Manchester	Estimate an increase of 2,500 per year (see below)					
No data available for Sunderland, Bradford, Tower Hamlets and Lambeth.						

27. In those authorities where there is a separate Welfare Rights Service provided by another department or voluntary organisation there tend to be no separate 'Welfare Rights' records for the social services department. In Knowsley officers were able to provide information on welfare rights referrals to one social work area covering 36% of the total borough population which showed such referrals running at 50 per month for three years. Although there has been little change over the last three years, a steady 50 referrals a month is still very significant. Otherwise *those authorities which are able to provide data show a very significant increase in welfare rights referrals over the survey period* confirming the findings in Newcastle, Sheffield and others referred to earlier.

28. *Those authorities with welfare rights and advisory services run by other departments are also able to identify increasing demands.*

29. Bradford Benefits Shops have been open since July 1982. The shops are a direct policy response to unemployment in the town and are run by the council's Unemployment Unit. The Unit conducted a benefits take-up survey in 1981 to assess the level of need for advice on benefits; the response was overwhelming and the Benefits Shops are the response to this demand. Demand on the new service has been extremely high.

30. Bradford Benefits Shops maintain computerised records of all callers and this includes employment status. These records show that during the first year ending July 1983, 67% of enquirers were unemployed. Enquiries are not specific to benefits alone but the vast majority are from people who are experiencing financial hardship. 24% of enquirers return for a second visit, of whom the majority are in chronic financial trouble. Demand continues to grow. The only debt work undertaken concerns fuel debts and 61% of enquiries of this nature during the period July 1982 to June 1984 were from unemployed people. The largest proportion of enquiries, 30%, are concerned with supplementary benefit.

31. Lambeth and Sunderland's experience is similar to Bradford's. In Lambeth the Health and Consumer Services Committee runs Consumer Advice Centres which are seen in Lambeth as one of several 'alternative strategies' developed in the late 1970s partly in response to growing unemployment. Lambeth Consumer Advice Centres offer shop-front style advice on benefits and financial matters. Approximately 50% of clients of the centres are unemployed. The service has been running for six years; in the early years fuel debts were the major problem but change in fuel board policy and practice locally have meant that these difficulties are resolved earlier. Housing rent arrears are now the most common problem.

32. Lambeth surveyed the users of their Consumer Advice Centres in November 1981 and found that 54.9% stated that they were unemployed; only 13% of those who did not work had someone else in their household who worked. 40.6% did not work, had no other wage earner in their household and were dependent on state benefits or another form of income such as occupational pension. An analysis of fuel debt problems referred to advice centres throughout the whole of 1980 revealed that 47.2% of cases concerning disconnections were dependent on supplementary benefit or unemployment benefit as sole source of income; and 55% of cases involving arrears were dependent on supplementary or unemployment benefit as a source of income.

33. Sunderland Borough Council fund Advice Centres. The view expressed by some officers of the Social Services Department was that they would prefer that the Welfare Rights and Financial Advice Service was run by their department because of the interrelation with other social work problems. Area social work teams in Sunderland are still dealing with increasing numbers of cases which primarily have a welfare rights/financial hardship element despite the existence of the advice centres. It is a matter of chance whether clients go to the social services department or advice centre — it depends if they are aware of the latter. Nevertheless area managers and social workers in Sunderland report that welfare rights and debt problems are the main growth areas in their work loads.

34. Similarly there is strong evidence of growing welfare rights/financial hardship work and a link with unemployment from the voluntary organisations operating on an agency basis in Coventry.

Table 5 — Welfare Rights Referrals to Voluntary Organisations Operating on an Agency Basis in Coventry

	1973/4	1978/9	1979/80	1980/1	1981/2	1982/3	% Change 1973/74–1982/83
Coventry CAB	1,003	U/A	U/A	U/A	2,123	2,246	+124%
Coventry Legal and Income Rights (CLAIR)	U/A	U/A	U/A	254	319	1,853 [1]	

[1]Estimate

35. In Coventry the Citizens Advice Bureau (CAB) and Coventry Legal and Income Rights (CLAIR) operate a welfare rights and advice service on behalf of the city council. Advice workers from CAB and CLAIR report a vast increase in welfare rights and debt-related work in the last eight years, so much so that there is now a large amount of unmet need. The majority of this work involves unemployed people on supplementary benefit. The advice work in both CAB and CLAIR has been totally distorted in favour of welfare rights/financial hardship work. Coventry CAB report that eight years ago advice work divided equally between the following four client groups:-

(i) Elderly
(ii) Unemployed
(iii) Sick
(iv) Single Parents

Now the unemployed group comprises 80% of all clients. Coventry CAB report that 50% of debt problems are from unemployed people.

36. A survey of social work referrals in Coventry conducted in 1979 found that 50% of all referrals had a welfare rights or debt content — one sixth were solely of a welfare rights/debt nature. The social services department send as many of these cases as possible to CLAIR or CAB. Social workers confirm that the proportion of referrals classified as welfare rights/debt cases has almost certainly increased from the 50% recorded in 1979. Despite the existence of CAB and CLAIR in Coventry there is still a lot of residual welfare rights work conducted by social workers and area managers report that this has increased noticeably in recent years.

37. *Area social work managers and social workers interviewed in each of the sample authorities confirmed a major increase in the number of social work cases involving primarily welfare rights.* This has occurred even in those authorities with a welfare rights service run outside the social services department. In these cases this is due to ignorance of the existence of the specialist services; or the fact that social services area offices are seen as accessible and local; or ignorance of who is responsible for what.

38. In many of the authorities in the sample the increase in welfare rights work by social workers is dramatic. For example, one social work intake team in Manchester report that four years ago there was only a trickle of intake cases related to benefits; now the major proportion of all new social work cases are of benefit-related nature.

39. In Manchester as a whole there are no regular records maintained on welfare rights referrals by the department's Welfare Rights Service. However, selective data from certain officers suggests markedly increased referral rates in the last 2-3 years. The Welfare Rights team estimate current global totals in excess of 2,500 new referrals dealt with by the team annually.

40. Not only did social workers interviewed point to a major increase in welfare rights referrals, they also identify that unemployment is a major contribution to this trend. For example, an area manager in Bradford commented that it was noticeable that more clients are long-term unemployed and more are dependent solely on supplementary benefit. In Manchester Welfare Rights Officers estimate that two thirds of all welfare rights referrals are from unemployed people and welfare rights referrals have increased directly with the period of greatest increase in unemployment.

Applications to Charities

41. Applications by social services departments to charities are good indicators of trends in financial problems amongst social services clients. In social work cases where there is a distinct financial requirement social workers often apply, on their behalf, to charities for funds to meet this need. Such arrangements equate to 'Section 1' payments or supplementary benefit single payments, and can cover payments for things materially affecting clients' lives from cookers to periods of convalescence. Not all authorities in the sample maintain records of applications to charities but the data available is shown in Table 6.

42. *Those authorities with data available show a very marked increase in general applications to charities — 30% and more during the period in which unemployment has increased at the greatest rate.* Interviews with area social work managers and social workers confirm a marked increase in applications to charities. An area manager in Coventry said that the trend in applications to charities was as significant as the increase in welfare rights referrals. Such cases occupy a lot of social work time as there is a large amount of form filling required.

Table 6 — Applications to Charities

	Year					% Change
Authority	**1978/9**	**1979/80**	**1980/1**	**1981/2**	**1982/3**	**1978/9 1982/3**
Tower Hamlets[1]	64	60	116	94	83	+30%
Manchester[2]	349	394	486	415	497	+42%
Coventry	264	288	233	344	356	+35%

[1]Information only available on successful applications.
[2]Applications to charities administered directly by the Department only.
No information for Sunderland, Bradford, Lambeth, Harrow or Knowsley.

43. In Manchester, in addition to a 40% increase in applications to departmentally administered charities, applications to external charities, although not recorded, are equally numerous.

44. Coventry have been able to identify the number of successful applicants to charities who were unemployed:-

Table 7 — Successful Applications for Charities Where Unemployment was the Prime Factor

	Year					% Change
	1978/79	**1979/80**	**1980/81**	**1981/82**	**1982/83**	**1978/79-1982/83**
Coventry						
Number	31	36	44	67	67	116%
Proportion	11.7%	12.5%	18.9%	19.5%	18.0%	

Conclusion

45. The evidence from the survey demonstrates a very significant upward trend in welfare rights and financial referrals, particularly for debt-related problems. Both mainstream social workers and specialist advice workers report ever increasing caseloads during the past five or six years. The only area of financial social services activity not to show a significant increase was section 1 payments; this is due to the financial pressure on local authorities leading to strict controls on this area of the budget. We found increases in welfare rights and financial hardship cases of around 50% on average over the last four or five years in the sample authorities. Generally two thirds of these were from unemployed people.

46. Most authorities see it as their duty to provide help with welfare rights and financial problems. A clear reasoning offered by social services departments for this is their duty to prevent children coming into care and to prevent these difficulties progressing into severe cases involving relationship problems and damaging family interaction. Such family casework involves considerably more social work time and effort than welfare rights and financial hardship cases. Furthermore those voluntary organisations providing advisory and welfare rights services are helping to stem social services demand in some areas by dealing with many of these cases rather than the local authority and preventing such cases developing into more serious family casework. A few authorities take an opposite view that welfare rights and financial cases are not part of their responsibility. Knowsley, for example, take the stance that given their limited resources, parameters have to be drawn to the cases they can deal with. They therefore place the emphasis on the 'traditional' cases involving families or the elderly, for example. Negotiations with fuel boards and the housing department have restricted the debt-related cases in their area to a minimum.

47. There was some disagreement about the role of advisory services provided outside social services departments. In most instances their work was seen as complementary to advice work by social workers. In one instance however the advice workers saw their activity as filling a complete void in the activity of the social services department.

48. Whatever administrative arrangements were operative there was a growing drain on local authority resources, primarily the social services budget. Although such cases are not as demanding or as lengthy as full family intervention cases they are still time-consuming and complex and can occur together with more complicated family-related problems.

Chapter 6
Aspects of Unemployment and Juvenile Crime

Recent Research

1. Evidence has been accumulating over the last decade of a close relationship between increasing unemployment and a rising rate of crime. Although a causal link has not and perhaps cannot be satisfactorily established, it is common sense to suppose that crime offers one way for the unemployed to obtain an income otherwise denied them. Unemployment also affords time for crime and the injustice of being unemployed in a society dominated by materialistic values may provide a very strong motive force for criminal behaviour.

2. There is statistical support for the existence of this relationship. Examining the effect of instability in the economy on criminal statistics over a 70 year period in England, Wales, Scotland, the United States and Canada, Brenner has argued that 'in general the rate of unemployment. . . . .shows significant and strong relationships to increases in trends of criminal statistical data for all major categories of crime and sources of statistics'. Using three economic indicators — unemployment, GNP and inflation — Brenner claimed that each was significant and that together they could account for more than 90% of the variation in the trends in criminal statistics.[1]

3. Recent questioning of such research has noted that recorded crime also rises during periods of economic growth, that criminality is as likely to cause unemployment as vice versa and that the peak age for criminal involvement, 15 years, is within the age of compulsory schooling before labour market involvement even begins.[2] It has also been argued that most of the rise in recorded crime may well be due to the increase in the proportion of offences recorded rather than in the number which occur. Brenner in particular has been criticised for basing his findings on recorded crime.[3]

4. Notwithstanding these debates, there is no escaping the fact that research studies of known offenders have 'repeatedly shown that somewhere in the region of 4 out of 10 were unemployed, a much higher proportion than that for the population as a whole'.[4] Such findings are especially relevant to the young. Phillips, Votey and Maxwell found that young people who were not working had significantly higher crime rates than those who were; they concluded that economic opportunity was a key factor in generating youthful crime and that changing labour market opportunities were sufficient to explain increasing crime rates for youth.[5] Later, McLintock suggested an intergenerational effect in that children of families where there is a history of unemployment are more likely to be delinquent than those with parents at work.[6]

5. Recent evidence continues to demonstrate the extent to which unemployment puts youth at risk of criminal involvement. A Rainer Foundation analysis of Juvenile Court Proceedings in Lewisham has found, for example, that over 62% of a sample of young offenders were unemployed and concludes that 'although the connection between crime and unemployment may not be direct and simple, it most certainly cannot be severed'.[7] NACRO, too, in its analysis of records for trainees in the second quarter of 1983 reported that about a third of trainees' fathers and a half of trainees' mothers were unemployed.[8] A survey of the National Association of Probation Officers of probation service clients showed their rate of unemployment to be 81%.[9]

6. Independent of the crime rate, unemployment is also closely related to custodial sentencing. In Britain, Box and Hale have argued that there is a virtual consensus that unemployment leads to an increase in imprisonment, with an increase of 1,000 in the number unemployed leading, on average, to 10 more people receiving prison sentences. This relationship is again particularly pronounced among the young. For every 1,000 young males, not 10 but 23 on average get sent to prison.[10] The DHSS exemplified this recently by noting 'The number of juveniles sent to detention centre and borstal has risen five-fold since 1965. Less than a fifth of the rise relates directly to increased offending; the remainder is caused by an increased tendency to give custodial sentences for almost all types of offence'.[11]

7. In some of the younger age groups court appearances and convictions are being reduced by an increase in police cautioning. Cautioning practices are known to vary widely from one area of the country to another but recent research has indicated that generally speaking in 1981 the cautioning rates for indictable offences approached 50% for juvenile males[12] (although remaining under 5% for young adult males). In Bradford declining figures for court appearances by juveniles are directly attributed to an increase in police cautioning. In fact it is most likely that cautioning statistics would provide the most reliable of guides to the incidence of juvenile crime in that particular area. This would by no means, however, be true of all the areas at which this survey looked.

8. Cautioning for less serious offences is greatly preferable to custodial sentencing, the results of which are often highly unsatisfactory, go no way towards reducing the crime rate and result in both personal deterioration and recidivism. If reducing the crime rate is a serious objective, however, policies other than cautioning or custody have to be explored, chief among which it has been argued is lowering unemployment. Since, however, a high rate of unemployment seems firmly set for the rest of the decade, with new jobs being largely of a part-time, service nature, such policies as there are offer little hope in this direction. Unfortunately, as NACRO points out 'hardship tends to make societies less tolerant, to look for scapegoats and for quick solutions rather than the best ones'.[13] Thus even sympathetic and constructive social policies are hard to come by.

9. In the light of the research linking unemployment and juvenile delinquency, it was decided that intermediate treatment, originally envisaged as a method of helping delinquents and as a preventative against custody, was an aspect of social service activities worth researching. This measure was initially elaborated in the Home Office White Paper, 'Children in Trouble' in 1968 and encompassed, though by no means defined, within the 1969 Children and Young Persons Act. A history of the development of IT in the 1970s has yet to be written, but its growth and evolution through the probation service and the personal social services has been sufficiently rapid and diverse to warrant the development of both monitoring processes[14] and a national survey into IT in the 1980s.[15]

10. Since 1969 the original concept of IT has undergone many changes, with child care theories and cultural deprivation theories broadening the original client group to include almost any children exhibiting 'undesirable', let alone 'criminal', behaviour. Within the AMA research project, this confusion surrounding IT, as well as a lack of information on IT schemes, has created predictable difficulties. As NACRO recorded in their research for CAYO (Community Alternatives for Young Offenders), 'Although police constabularies, the Home Office and the DHSS require statistical information on juvenile offenders and children in care annually from the relevant agencies and the courts, this same information is not always readily available at a local level'.[16] All the same the information collected and interviews obtained in this survey do suggest some interesting hypotheses about the needs of young people in areas of high unemployment and, if nothing else, indicate potential channels for future research.

The Survey

Places and Plans for Intermediate Treatment

11. The authorities were asked about the numbers of teenagers placed in IT centres between 1978-79 and 1982-83. Although information on both over 16-year-olds and under 16-year-olds was requested, it was not possible to obtain much data according to age. The prime reason for this was that by far the majority of those attending IT courses are under 16; they are also by and large school truants, for whom IT has become an alternative form of schooling when full-time or a supplement to schooling when part-time. One interviewee went so far as to state emphatically that there was no point in attempting to put over-16s onto IT as they simply would not attend nor think of it as worthwhile. Given this stance, many of our subsequent questions on the ways in which IT might be helping or might be planned in the future to prepare young people for employment were not seen as relevant by some officers. It was stated that other agencies would be concerned with employment, whereas IT's major concern was to encourage youngsters to review their delinquency and channel their energies in other more acceptable directions.

12. Table 1 records the information obtained on numbers in IT centres in the authorities concerned:

Table 1 — Number of People at IT Centres, 31st March

	1979	1980	1981	1982	1983
Coventry	—	—	(81/82) 153	(82/83) 147	(83/84) 141
Lambeth	—	352	528	573	—
Harrow	—	16	16	8	—
Tower Hamlets	39	49	64	100	134
Knowsley	2	2	0	3	0
Manchester	—	—	48	118	188
Sunderland	—	—	—	—	—
Bradford	—	—	—	—	165

(A dash may indicate either no facilities, or no figures available)

These incomplete figures, reveal no discernible pattern of IT response amongst these authorities. Only three, Lambeth, Tower Hamlets and Manchester show an increase in provision. Coventry, at a fairly high level of service, shows a slight drop. Harrow and Knowsley with minimal provision also show a drop. Sunderland had no facilities of this kind during the survey period and Bradford supplied figures for 1983 only. Such inconsistencies are unsurprising given the diversity of IT provision.

13. A second question asked for figures for the number of supervision orders with an IT requirement made by Juvenile Courts. These figures as shown in Table 2, are more consistent, showing in all cases except Manchester and Coventry a downward trend in the number of supervision orders made incorporating an IT requirement. These figures do not, however, show where IT is being used on a voluntary basis rather than as a requirement with a precise meaning in law. Increasingly social services departments are not recommending IT requirements as these are expensive and instead are suggesting voluntary IT.

Table 2 — Number of Supervision Orders with an IT Requirement

	1978/79	1979/80	1980/81	1981/82	1982/83
Coventry	50	47	48	45	55
Lambeth	33	35	29	45	30
Harrow	—	20	16	19	13
Tower Hamlets	figures not available				
Knowsley	0	1	1	2	0
Manchester	26	33	45	62	73
Sunderland	56 ('78)	59 ('79)	.....101.....		50 ('83)
Bradford	137	139	162	143	88

Bradford was able to show how supervision with IT had declined within social services and the probation service, although with the social services contribution being much more markedly reduced. Is this indicative of a change in magistrates' policies? Possibly fewer supervision orders are being made in areas where in the social services themselves IT is not seen as an alternative to custody. In Manchester, for example, a recent effort with NACRO support to develop IT deliberately as an alternative to custody could account for the increased figure. On the other hand, it could simply be that IT requirements are not being recommended by social services departments and probation officers, either because of a lack of resources, or because faith in IT is weakening, or because of other alternatives for young offenders.

14. An attempt has been made to compare this information with that available in Home Office statistics on court appearances and sentencing. Table 3 shows the percentage of 14-16 year-old males (the main IT client group) who from those found guilty received custodial sentences rather than fines or supervision, between 1979 and 1983.[17] Areas where a lower percentage of offenders received custodial sentences (Coventry, Lambeth and Tower Hamlets) exhibit a stronger commitment to IT according to our placement figures than do areas like Knowsley and Sunderland where levels of custodial sentencing are generally higher and have been exceptionally high in the past.

15. On a very speculative note, it appears that there may be three types of relationships existing between courts and social services departments with consequently diverging implications for the young people found guilty of crimes. First there are authorities where magistrates, aware of the drawbacks of custody, are willing and more importantly able to find an alternative to custody in local IT schemes; these, including Coventry, Lambeth and Tower Hamlets, exhibit a high level of investment in IT and relatively low custodial sentencing. Secondly, there are those like Sunderland and Knowsley where IT provision is minimal and custodial sentencing remains high because there is no alternative. Thirdly, there are those like Manchester and Bradford where although IT provision is being extended, it has been accustomed to focus on younger children and so has provided the courts with no alternative for older children. This is no more than a hypothetical pattern as present evidence is too slight to confirm it properly, but interviews and general impressions lend it support. Unfortunately statistical corroboration will be hard to come by given the inadequacy of information and the fact that official statistics, taken from the petty sessional information, do not coincide with local authority boundaries.

Table 3 — Proportion of 14-16 year-old Males Found Guilty of Indictable Offences and Receiving Custodial Sentences 1979-1983

	1979	1980	1981	1982	1983
Coventry	22.8	17.2	15.1	11.5	10.4
Sunderland	16.5	15.9	20.4	16.5	16.6
Knowsley	32.1	23.1	21.1	18.1	17.6
Manchester	13.1	16.2	14.7	15.2	14.4
Bradford	10.6	12.8	12.9	9.9	12.1
Lambeth	12.8	15.4	11.0	11.1	11.3
Tower Hamlets (East)	11.2	5.5	12.2	12.3	11.0
Harrow	16.4	14.1	12.5	8.7	14.3

16. Although local authorities are encouraged under the 1969 Act to develop IT as an alternative to custody, there is no financial incentive for them to do so. In fact the reverse is the case, as delinquents being sent to a detention centre will be paid for by the prison department, whereas those on IT must be paid for by social services out of the general personal social services budget. This may be one good reason why local authorities may choose to direct their IT schemes at children under 14 for whom custody is generally not possible, rather than at older teenagers. Looked at in broad terms, however, the consequences of this financial restraint are widespread, resulting not only in more older teenagers in custody but also in greater national cost. It is vastly cheaper to run an IT centre than a detention centre or other forms of custodial treatment. Arguably it is also a much more practical proposition in terms of value to the individual and ultimate success — though without proper proof this does still remain an argument.

Intermediate Treatment and Unemployment

17. In areas of high unemployment it has already been argued that juvenile delinquency is likely to become of increasing concern. Statistically in local authority areas this is sometimes hard to substantiate as changing police practices such as the increase in cautioning already mentioned or concentration on more serious crimes may actually lead to a drop in convictions at a time of rising unemployment. Nevertheless professional opinion as well as previously quoted research underlines the likelihood that young people in trouble are likely both to come from families where unemployment is prevalent and to have difficulty in finding employment themselves. A count of young people on an IT register in Tower Hamlets for example, suggested that 50% came from families where the breadwinner was unemployed and, if single parents had been included, the figure would probably have been higher still. Because of this a series of related questions were put to the authorities in this survey on the estimated impact of unemployment on young people and the attempts being made through IT projects to do something about this.

18. Universally the effect of unemployment on the young was described as devastating. In areas where youth unemployment was both high and rising a sense of hopelessness was judged to be contributing to further crime, solvent and alcohol abuse and drug-taking. Changing these undesirable behaviour patterns was made doubly difficult by the absence of job opportunities and relevant work experience. Most IT centres were making some efforts towards helping older teenagers with filling out application forms, developing confidence and effective self- presentation in interviews and so forth. Few, however, were actively engaged in creating work experience opportunities or helping young people develop marketable skills. Again, this was often because the centres were dealing with young teenagers, not school leavers.

19. There were however exceptions to this general pattern. In Tower Hamlets in the IT day-care project, young people in their last year of schooling are prepared for employment through work experience in local workshops or by inclusion in courses in local colleges of education. Proposals have also been drawn up for a craft/carpentry workshop to draw on any potential among day-care and other IT members which might enable them to find employment in the building or allied trades. Total cost, including tools and extra security for the craft workshop, has been estimated at £1,000 with weekly sessional fees of approximately £25. In Sunderland some structured help is given at Milestones Intensive IT project and also, in conjunction with the YMCA, there are plans to initiate a new IT scheme for unemployed school leavers who need organised daytime activities. Such activities are however not directly aimed at employability but at developing creativity and self-esteem. In Bradford three schemes encompassing 29 young people contain an element of employment preparation and a new centre opened in 1983 has been specially developed with this in mind. In Coventry, a joint working party has been formed with the police, probation service and social services (CITA) and is planning special schemes, some indirectly related to unemployment.

20. In Lambeth probably the widest range of IT schemes amongst the authorities exists with several closely related in their aims to future employment. Included are IT centres with work experience schemes and office training and the CAVE project, aimed at equipping a group of 14-16 year-olds with the necessary skills for seeking employment on leaving school. In the CAVE school, the children who are all 14-16 year-olds with long-term truancy records from local schools, are given a programme of education up to public examination level with appropriate group work designed to promote co-operation and clarity of expression and work experience. CAVE is now planning a project for 36 16-19 year-olds who are unemployed and requiring basic education. Also of interest here is the Lambeth Community Service Scheme which offers work and social experience to those over 16 who have been in community homes or in care. Most experience is obtained in old people's homes, day nurseries etc where the service scheme has links established over several years. There is little rapport with business or local industry, however, and attempts to establish links have not worked.

21. Lambeth has clearly stated the objectives contained within its IT services. It aims 'to maintain the integrity of the family and prevent reception into care on all grounds; to reduce delinquent behaviour and minimise its anti-social quality and the degree of risk to local people; to provide credible alternatives to inappropriate custodial and residential placements and to seek to help youngsters in difficulty to lead self-fulfilling and fruitful lives in the community'.[18] In most of the authorities in this survey, lack of IT facilities makes the pursuit of such objectives an impossibility and, even in those with a higher provision of places, lack of emphasis on employability, coupled with the dearth of realistic employment prospects, puts such objectives out of reach.

Conclusion

22. Although the evidence obtained was patchy and incomplete, it did highlight the diversity and inconsistency known to exist in IT provision in social services departments. It also showed a general decline in the number of supervision orders being made with an IT requirement in five of the eight authorities, though this did not imply a drop in voluntary IT. Lack of IT provision for older teenagers and the lack of schemes directed at their employability is striking. It seems that for older, difficult teenagers, or for those in trouble there is little help to be found in social services departments. Their future, therefore, apart from the brief respite offered by YTS, seems most likely to be divided between periods in detention and unemployment.

Chapter 7
Social Work Referrals: A Survey of Employment Status

Background

1. To supplement the limited data on employment status of social services clients it was decided to take a one month 'snapshot' survey of social work referrals in each of the sample authorities, establishing the employment status of clients referred during that period. The object was not to gather retrospective data but to identify the proportion of clients who were unemployed or who had unemployed people in their household, including also the nature of their unemployment. It was hoped to ascertain whether unemployment is a feature of a significant proportion of new social services cases and their families, and to identify the problems about which they were seeking help.

Other Studies

2. There have been other studies of social work referrals and unemployment, although these have been at a local level. Notable is Nash's survey in Peterborough of referrals to a social services team.[1] Nash compared the level of unemployment in his client population with that in the total area population and examined social services problems manifested by unemployed people. Nash collected employment details of all referrals to the reception team during one month and found that of those clients who could work — i.e. the 'economically active' — a very large proportion (66%) were unemployed. This compared with 12% in Peterborough's total

'economically active' population. Similarly if cases were taken instead of clients, 32% of cases involved either unemployed individuals or families with an unemployed individual within them. In 80% of cases involving unemployed clients, financial and housing problems were paramount.

3. A survey was also conducted by Strathclyde Regional Social Work Department on the impact of unemployment arising from the closure of the Talbot car plant at Linwood.[2] The social work area office in Renfrew monitored the change in referrals involving ex-Talbot workers. This revealed increases in the proportion of clients unemployed to the point where only 1 in 10 were employed, and that the most common cases involved financial and fuel debt problems.

Methods

4. The sample authorities agreed in principle to participate and after consultation with them an agreed questionnaire was designed. The questionnaire was to be completed by social workers for each new social work referral during the one month period — in this case September 1984. The sample authorities were asked to select one or more social work areas to handle the questionnaire, representing a resident population of 20,000 to 50,000 people. In some authorities this required two or three social work areas. Authorities also attempted to select an area which was not unrepresentative of the authority as a whole. This was achieved in Coventry, for example, by selecting three contrasting areas; one an inner-city area, one an area with a high ethnic minority population and a third representing a more prosperous area. The areas used by the sample authorities were:-

Authority	*Areas*
Sunderland	North Eastern
Manchester	Central
Lambeth	—
Harrow	Middle team, central area
Bradford	Keighley
Tower Hamlets	—
Knowsley	Kirkby
Coventry	Foleshill, Canley, Bell Green

5. Common definitions had to be constructed for 'client', 'referral' and 'new'. 'Referral/enquiry' was defined as 'a person or persons who seek, or are referred for, information or assistance in respect of whom a member of the social services staff has to ascertain some background information about social circumstances'. 'New' was defined as 'all referrals or enquiries seen in the four-week period in question'. This precluded all referrals/enquiries begun before this period. Those recorded as unemployed included only those 'actively seeking work' by which we meant only those either registered for employment or those who would like to work given the opportunity. We recognised the unsatisfactory nature of this last categorisation, but did not wish to complicate the recording process by adding further qualifications. One result of this has been an in-built assumption that amongst those then classified as 'not seeking work' there are many, particularly women, who would work under different circumstances.[3]

6. Consultation was necessary too in constructing a list of 'main presenting problems' in order to classify the type of referral or problem dealt with. Each authority submitted its own classifications and a common list was synthesised from this.

7. The questionnaire used by social workers in the survey begins by establishing the essential common facts about the referred person, that is age and sex, and then seeks the 'main presenting problem'. Next the questionnaire goes on to ascertain the employment status of the referred person, whether employed, retired, in full-time education or unemployed. If they are unemployed the questionnaire seeks information about the duration of unemployment. Following on from this, the questionnaire next seeks information about the employment status of other members of the referred person's family together with duration of unemployment if appropriate.

8. The month chosen for the survey, September, represented a period not adversely distorted by seasonal influences. One of the area offices in Coventry was unable to conduct the survey in September but did so in October instead. We do not consider that this affected the results significantly.

9. After discussing the survey with their relevant social work teams, Tower Hamlets and Lambeth for internal reasons were unable to complete the exercise. The remaining authorities successfully recorded all referrals in the survey period with the exception of

Sunderland, who due to the unexpected pressures of the miners' strike, could survey only 25% of referrals. Nevertheless this 25% was representative of all referrals to the area team during the survey period. In total nearly 800 referrals in six authorities were recorded.

Description of the Sample

10. 796 completed referral forms were received. Of these 304 referred to men and 480 to women. Table 1 below gives the full age and sex details of the sample:-

Table 1 — Age at Last Birthday and Sex of Referred Persons

	Male	Female	Male & Female	No Reply	Total
Under 16	20	10			30 (3.8%)
15 to under 18	11	14			25 (3.1%)
18 to under 25	26	54			80 (10.1%)
25 to under 40	53	119	1		173 (21.7%)
40 to under 65	83	85	2		170 (21.4%)
65 and over	95	178	2	2	277 (34.8%)
No reply	16	20	2	3	41 (5.2%)
TOTAL	304 (38.2%)	480 (60.3%)	7 (0.9%)	5 0.6%)	796 (100.0%)

Number of missing observations = 0

11. As can be seen the largest age group is that over 65. As this group will be primarily retired and therefore not part of the job market, we have discounted this group of 277 from our analysis of the unemployed. The survey found that of the total referrals 53.1% of referred persons were heads of households and 14.3% were spouses, 6% were under 18 and 8.4% other adults in households. The majority of heads of households (40%) were aged over 65 and the next largest group (24%) aged 40-65.

12. The survey attempted to focus more broadly than on the employment status of the referred person to include both long-term unemployed and the employment status of other adults in the household in order to explore the concept of family unemployment.

13. The survey examined whether there were any waged or unwaged adults in the referred person's household. Table 2 below gives this information according to age of the referred person:-

Table 2 — Waged and Unwaged Adults in Referred Persons Households by Age

AGE	Unwaged Adult	Waged Adult	Total
Under 16	24	6	30 5.7%
16 to under 18	17	8	25 (4.8%)
18 to under 25	64	16	80 (15.4%)
25 to under 40	121	52	173 (33.3%)
40 to under 65	137	33	170 (32.8%)
No reply	36	5	41 7.9%)
TOTAL	399 (76.9%)	120 (23.1%)	519 (100.0%)

Number of missing observations = 0

14. Therefore 76.9% of referred persons aged under 65 had no waged adult in their household. This does not mean that all are unemployed as this group will include those who do not consider themselves available for work, for example chronically sick persons, those describing themselves as 'housewives' or those in full-time education.

15. The survey revealed that long-term unemployment — defined as those unemployed for more than one year — was a common feature in the households of referred persons of all sizes. This is demonstrated in Table 3 below:-

Table 3 — Age of Referred Persons by Long-Term Unemployed Adult in the Household

Age of Referred Person	No Long-Term Unemployment	Long-Term Unemployment	Total
Under 16	25	5	30 (5.8%)
16 to under 18	17	8	25 (4.8%)
18 to under 25	48	32	80 (15.4%)
25 to under 40	119	54	173 (33.3%)
40 to under 65	131	39	170 (32.8%)
No reply	36	5	41 (7.9%)
TOTAL	376 (72.4%)	143 (27.6%)	519 (100.0%)

Number of Missing Observations = 0

16. Nearly 28% of the households of referred persons contained long-term unemployed adults. The concentration was in the households of referred persons aged 18 to 25 (40%) and 25 to 40 (31%).

17. Perhaps the most distinctive finding relates to the employment circumstances of the referred persons themselves. Table 4 below describes whether or not the referred person is in paid employment.

Table 4 — Referred Persons in Paid Employment

	Frequency	Percent
Referred Person in Paid Employment	61	7.7%
Referred Person not in Paid Employment	715	89.8%
No Reply	20	2.8%
TOTAL	796	100.0%

From a sample of 796 social work cases only 61 (7.7%) were in paid employment. These results, if typical of metropolitan authorities, suggest that few employed people seek help from social services departments.

Household Composition and Unemployment

18. Out of the total 796 referrals 30 were people under 16, of which 24 (80%) had no adult in their household in paid employment. One of these was a retired head of household with the remaining heads of household either unemployed or classified as at home but not seeking work. The majority of the under-16 referrals had only one adult with no spouse; 80% had no spouse in addition to the head of household. Households with no waged adult showed a much higher incidence of lone parents than those with waged adults — 91.7% against 33.3%. Therefore in child referrals (under 16) there was a high incidence of both unemployment and lone parents.

19. Of the 766 referred persons over 16, 632 (82.5%) had no adult in their household in paid employment. 257 of these were over 65 and can therefore be discounted in terms of unemployment. Table 5 below outlines the employment status of the remainder.

Table 5 —Age and Employment Status of Referred Persons Aged 16-65 in Households with no Working Adult

	EMPLOYMENT STATUS					
Age	Unemployed	Retired	Education	Not seeking work	No reply	Total
16–under 18	7	—	5	4	1	17
18–under 25	34	—	2	26	2	64
25–under 40	46	—	1	72	2	121
40–under 65	35	27	—	71	4	137
No reply	13	9	3	7	4	36
TOTAL	135 (36%)	36 (10%)	11 (3%)	180 (48%)	13 (3%)	375 (100%)

36% therefore described themselves as unemployed under our common description, but a further 48% were 'at home but not seeking work' and it is not possible to predict how many of these are 'housewives', disabled and chronically sick, who may in better times realistically seek work.

20. A similar pattern emerged for those referred persons aged 16-65 who had working adults in the household, 24 or 23% were unemployed themselves and 20% not seeking work. If this is added to the data in Table 5 the proportion of all referred persons of working age unemployed in the sample is 33%.

21. There were 161 referred persons in the sample aged over 16 who described themselves as unemployed. Table 6 below identifies the position in their household of this group and whether there are any other adults in this household in paid employment.

Table 6 — Referred Persons aged over 16 and Unemployed — Position in household and waged adults in the household

UNEMPLOYED REFERRED PERSONS AGED OVER 16			
Position in Household of Unemployed Referred Person	**Other Adults in Paid Employment in Household**	**No Other Adults in Paid Employment in Household**	**Total**
Head of Household	11	90	101 (63%)
Spouse/Cohabitee	6	11	17 (11%)
Child Under 18	3	5	8 (5%)
Other Adult	4	19	23 (14%)
Head of Household and Spouse	—	2	2 (1%)
No Reply	—	10	10 (6%)
Total	24 (15%)	137 (85%)	161 (100%)

56% of the unemployed referred persons were heads of household and had no other adult in paid employment in their household. Whereas only 7% of the referred persons were spouses or cohabitees with no other adult in the household in paid employment. *This suggests that the majority of the social services referrals in this sample are either unemployed single parent families or households with widespread unemployment.*

Duration of Unemployment

22. As established above, of the 766 referred persons aged over 16 in the sample, 161 or 33% of those of working age were unemployed. We collected data on the duration of unemployment of this group and this is presented in Table 7 according to whether there are any other adults in the household in paid employment.

Table 7 — Duration of Referred Person's Unemployment according to other adults in household in paid employment

Duration of Unemployment	No Other Working Adult in Household	Other Working Adult in Household	Total
Less than 3 months	16	2	18 (11%)
3 months — less than 6 months	6	3	9 (6%)
6 months — less than 1 year	12	8	20 (12%)
1 year — less than 2 years	27	10	37 (23%)
More than 2 years	54	1	55 (34%)
Periodically for more than 2 years	6	—	6 (4%)
Other	1	—	1 (1%)
No reply/don't know	15	—	15 (9%)
TOTAL	137	24	161 (100%)

This table demonstrates that the majority of unemployed referrals suffered long-term unemployment. Over 50% of the referred persons had long-term unemployment of between one and two years or for more than two years. *This indicates a high incidence of sustained and severely long-term unemployment amongst the referred persons in this survey.* The trend was similar in both households with other working adults and those without other working adults, however the households which had other working adults did not have the same high incidence of very long-term unemployment of over two years.

The Main Presenting Problems and Their Relationship to Unemployment

23. A considerable length of time was spent initially in this exercise defining a set of 'presenting problems' acceptable for use by all the authorities concerned. These 'presenting problems' had to have meaning primarily for the social workers filling in the referrals forms, and to be defined within the frames of reference commonly used. As such they were to some extent subjective. The final list was an amalgam of the categories found to be widely used already. Overlapping categories were removed or combined. In all, 25 categories were selected, with space reserved for another three options. In practice, however, it was found that all these could, for purposes of this analysis, be readily subsumed under six headings:-

1. *Financial/Material Needs*
   Financial
   Fuel Debts
   Material Needs
   Accommodation
   Homelessness

2. *Handicaps*
   Physical Disability
   Mental Handicap
   Transport/Mobility
   Physical Illness/Frailty
   Self Care

3. *Child Related*
   Criminal Offence
   Child Neglect
   Physical Injury to Child
   Solvent Abuse
   Marital Problem
   Notification of Intention to Adopt
   Behaviour/Attendance at School

4. *Family/Environment*
   Behaviour in Home
   Behaviour in Community
   Family Behaviour
   Death in Family
   Social Isolation

5. *Psychological*
   Emotional Disturbance
   Mental Illness

6. *Employment*
   Employment

24. Amongst the 796 referrals recorded, 'first problems' were thus identified:

Table 8 — First Presenting Problem

	Frequency	Percent
Financial/material	356	44.7%
Handicaps	277	34.8
Child related	67	8.4
Family environment	44	5.5
Psychological	33	4.1
Employment	11	1.4
No reply	8	1.0
TOTAL	796	100.00%

25. Clearly financial and material difficulties are identified as the most urgent, with 'employment problems' identified as negligible. Whilst this may seem surprising amongst clients exhibiting a high level of unemployment, it is not without its parallels. Tower Hamlets, which did not participate in this survey, but runs its own annual referrals exercise, has also recorded employment as negligible in terms of importance as a presenting problem. Neither, in our own survey, did 'employment' appear as a significant, or even second, third or fourth presenting problem. That is to say people did not come to seek help over employment.

26. When, however, those referred persons primarily experiencing financial and material difficulties were checked for employment status the following was the result:-

Table 9 — First Presenting Problem and Employment of Referred Person Aged over 18

First Problem	Employment Yes	Employment No	No Reply	Total
Financial/Material	35	302	2	339
Handicaps	6	251	14	271
Child Related	8	40	1	49
Family/Environment	5	27	1	33
Psychological	3	28	1	32
Employment	—	11	—	11
No Reply	1	5	—	6
TOTAL	58	664	19	741
%	7.8	89.6	2.6	100%

27. A more detailed analysis of employment status demonstrates that of those not in employment, 95 were unemployed and 113 classed as 'not seeking work'. Some degree of unemployment may be reasonably anticipated in this latter group. The rest were either retired or a few in education. As the following table shows it is clearly the unemployed and those 'not seeking work' who mostly experience financial and material difficulties.

Table 10 — Employment Status of Referred Persons Over 18 and First Presenting Problem

First Problem	Unemployed	Retired	Education	Not Seeking Work	No Reply
Financial/Material	95	89	4	113	38
Handicaps	19	175	1	56	20
Child Related	15	1	5	19	9
Family/Environment	4	9	—	13	7
Psychological	6	12	—	10	4
Employment	9	—	—	2	—
No Reply	3	2	—	—	1
TOTAL	151	288	10	213	79
%	20.4%	38.9%	13%	28.7%	10%

Together this group encompass 49.1% (nearly half) of all the referrals and account for about two-thirds of those in financial or material difficulties.

28. The conclusion drawn from this is that the *financial and material difficulties of many referred persons are closely related to unemployment or not being in work. Employment is probably not identified as a primary presenting problem because it is not the issue on which individuals seek help, yet it is in fact of major significance.*

29. Furthermore, amongst those defined as 'unemployed', poverty clearly increases with the duration of unemployment. Of the 95 unemployed people with financial and material difficulties, 10 had been unemployed for between six months and one year, 21 for between one year and two years and 36 for over two years.

30. Finally it is evident that *all* the presenting problems occur much more frequently in homes where there is no waged adult. If we remove those referrals who are retired from the 'no waged-adult' tabulation, we find the following:-

Table 11 — Presenting Problem of Working Age Referrals by any Waged Adult in the Household

	No Waged Adult	Waged Adult	Total	
Financial/Material	183	67	250	(55%)
Handicaps	64	32	96	(21%)
Child Related	36	12	48	(11%)
Family/Environment	18	6	24	(5%)
Psychological	12	6	18	(4%)
Employment	9	2	11	(2%)
No Reply	3	1	4	(1%)
TOTAL	325	126	451	
%	73%	27%	100%	

Conclusion

31. Although not a random sample of social work referrals, it seems reasonable to suppose that the 796 referrals considered in this survey are typical of those who regularly approach social services departments for help. Rather than overstating the case of unemployment as a cause of need, this survey may however have understated it — firstly because the two inner-London areas of Lambeth and Tower Hamlets were unable to participate and, secondly, because time and practicality did not permit any refinement of the 'not seeking work' categorisation.

32. Our figures suggest that social work referrals are highly likely to be persons either retired, not seeking work or unemployed; and in any event primarily 'unwaged'. 33% of the referred persons of working age in the sample were unemployed according to our definition. This is significantly higher than the average unemployment rate for the sample as a whole of 17%. In addition 30 of the referred persons were under 16 of which 80% had no waged adult in the household. Their problems were closely linked to their employment status, with financial and material difficulties most prominent amongst the unemployed and those not seeking work. These problems are more likely to occur, moreover, as the duration of unemployment increases.

33. This survey pin-points the need for a more systematic and refined analysis of the pattern of social services referrals. If more were known about this pattern, resources could be more effectively distributed. Secondly, our study underlines the perceptions that social workers hold of their clients' problems. These focus, understandably, on the presenting problem — be it mental illness or financial hardship — and not on underlying socio-economic causes.

Chapter 8
Unemployed People and Social Services Departments: Main Findings of the Survey and Some Implications for Social Policy

The Common Experience of Unemployment

1. This broadly based survey has attempted to discover and describe for the first time the impact of unemployment on personal social services' activities in selected metropolitan authorities. The eight metropolitan authorities areas chosen — Coventry, Bradford, Sunderland, Knowsley, Manchester, Tower Hamlets, Lambeth and Harrow — are linked by their common experience of unemployment which today affects between 15% and 30% per cent of their working-age population. Only Harrow, selected as a contrast to the other authorities, has maintained relatively low unemployment of approximately 6%. Even there economic change has resulted in some groups being disproportionately affected.

2. *These areas typify the different aspects of unemployment nationally*: Coventry, Bradford and Manchester represent previously affluent areas suddenly and disastrously affected by unemployment for the first time in two generations; Sunderland is an area in which persistent unemployment has suddenly escalated; Knowsley is comparable with many 'outer estate' areas built since World War Two in which the sudden unemployment has contributed to conditions even worse than those of the 'inner city' environments of which Lambeth and Tower Hamlets are typical; Harrow is similar to many other suburbs in which unemployment has been caused by the uneven change from light industrial work to service sector employ-

ment. *In all these areas, however, unemployment has provoked or intensified a common range of problems, making these authorities comparable on a number of issues.*

3. The six social service activities studied include those for *mentally and physically handicapped people, for children in care and leaving care, for mentally ill people, for children at risk, for juvenile delinquents and for families with financial problems. These groups are particularly vulnerable during any recession.* This study shows how some of the problems they encounter when unemployment increases give rise to measurable and serious additional demands on local authority social services.

Increased Demand for the Social Services Resulting from Unemployment

4. In the six social service activities with which the AMA survey has been concerned, accumulated evidence in the whole sample has revealed increasing and intensifying needs that are not, given current resources and practices, being adequately met. As the various chapters of this report demonstrate, these needs are decisively related to the rapid and recent growth of unemployment. As a result of this, centres for the handicapped are oversubscribed and unable in some cases to offer any facilities for the less severely handicapped who can no longer obtain work.[1] In children's homes staffing levels and rotas are inadequate to cope with the increased presence of unemployed young people during the day; children leaving care are more than ever before finding difficulties in living independently when faced with immediate and long-term unemployment with its attendant financial and psychological problems.[2] *Referrals of mentally ill people to social services departments are increasing* not only because of the progressive transfer of patients from hospital into the community in line with current community care policy but also because of the stresses imposed on family life by unemployment. At the same time, *people recovering from mental illness are being faced with a rehabilitation process in which work cannot play its vital part.*[3] Child abuse in areas of high unemployment appears to be increasing.[4] *Older delinquents are excluded from intermediate treatment* and, notwithstanding the Youth Training Scheme (YTS) opportunities, are being offered little help towards

future employability. For such young people the short duration of YTS is inadequate when what is needed is support and encouragement over a considerable period towards a stable and crime-free adult life.[5] *Debts of all kinds are proliferating amongst unemployed people*; welfare rights officers and social workers cannot cope with the increasing numbers of individuals requiring help with the complex social security system and meeting bills for fuel and rent.[6] New referrals to the social services, apart from the elderly whose numbers are increasing, are therefore very likely either to be unemployed or to be members of families where unemployment is a significant factor in the problems to be dealt with.[7] *In the most difficult cases not only the breadwinner but spouse and teenage children may all be be unemployed, bringing into focus the depressing syndrome of 'family unemployment'.*

5. Young people and ethnic minorities seem to be especially at risk. Social workers report evidence of mental distress, drug-taking, alcoholism and delinquency, reflecting the plight of young people joining the ranks of the long-term unemployed. This was graphically illustrated in this survey by those interviewed about children leaving care, a group of social service users for whom employment prospects are at their bleakest. For such young people, not only is suitable accommodation in a familiar area felt to be necessary, but also regular contact with social workers for help with managing bills and those domestic tasks which children in care often do not learn in the same way as children in families.[8] There is also an urgent need to develop facilities easing the transition from living in a home to total independence.[9] This is especially important now that for most of these young people employment,around which both life and finances may be structured, is so precarious.[10] One result of all this has been *a marked increase in the demands being placed on staff in children's homes and on other social workers, with a clear need also for increased after-care provision and social services support for young people leaving care without work.*

6. Although unemployment statistics for the ethnic minorities are no longer being collected by the Department of Employment, levels of youth unemployment were reportedly very high for Afro/Caribbeans in Lambeth and for Asians in Lambeth, Tower Hamlets, Bradford and Harrow. There was also evidence from social workers to suggest that extended family relationships amongst Asians could be under threat as well, with an as yet undocumented increase in mental distress amongst Asian parents, possibly even to the point of child abuse and suicide. Such evidence must also be considered in the light of known racial harassment and discrimination, a factor with which this survey has not been directly concerned but which was frequently raised in interviews.

7. *People living in certain areas have also proved to be particularly vulnerable to unemployment.* Parts of the 'inner city' have long been characterised by their low quality of life and lack of employment opportunities. Groups living in such areas of which the survey areas of Lambeth and Tower Hamlets are typical were, as expected, particularly at risk. No less so, however, were those living on the outer estates of major cities — areas to be found in and around Knowsley, Bradford and Sunderland — where the recession has killed economic and industrial activity so effectively that communities built up in the 1950s and '60s have now been reduced to depressed and virtually bankrupt shadows of their former selves. In Bradford, for example, it is argued that the image of the inner city as the only badly off area in the district is a myth, with unemployment in both the inner city and outer council estates averaging over 20%. We are supported in this by a recent CES document which highlighted this by looking at the impoverishment of four outer-estate areas, noting their near barter-type economy and their extensive reliance on social security and the social services for survival.[11]

Recognising the Effects of Unemployment in Social Services Departments

8. The extent to which unemployment has affected the social services has only very recently become a matter for public concern. Even in the social services themselves, the aggregate effects of unemployment appear not to have been fully appreciated by social service workers and their managers. Traditional social work perceptions may have led some social workers to assume that it was those with problems who became unemployed and not unemployment that created problems needing social work intervention or social services support. Others may have been prevented from recognising the effects of unemployment by the day-to-day necessity of concentrating on individual cases. As our interviews revealed, *the generalised effect of economic recession and unemployment is often not perceived by social services staff*, or where perceived is not translated into their daily work for a number of reasons. This goes some way towards explaining, for example, why 'unemployment' rarely features as a 'presenting problem' category in social work case records. The 'individualistic' approach may also partly explain the lack of information on the employment status of the users of the social services or of those upon whom the users were dependent. Such may also account for the minor importance attached to unemployment and changes in the local economy in forward planning for the social services.

9. Many instances were found in which data on unemployment was not kept because, presumably, its importance was not appreciated. Information was often unobtainable, for example, on the users of day centres and ATCs, on the numbers of older teenagers in care receiving allowances for board and lodging, on juvenile offenders referred to social services departments and, above all, on the employment status of clients. This latter had serious implications for our own research.

10. Because of the way in which information on users is collected in different local authorities, the balance of research findings in this survey has been uneven, both in terms of the six social services activities investigated and in terms of the ratio of quantitative to qualitative information. Whereas in some authorities usable quantitative material was available on resources for handicapped and mentally ill people, retrospective data was almost totally lacking on children in care or juvenile delinquents. Financial material was not as available as expected, partly due to a lack of liaison between social services departments and their finance departments in this respect. As a result this survey has relied heavily on the 52 interviews conducted with 73 social services officers. As a direct consequence of the lack of data about unemployment it was also decided to pursue the month long referrals survey to provide some firsthand quantitative material. Our work has indicated that there is no doubt that unemployment is a significant influence on the nature and volume of social services departments' work at the present time. Social services departments might therefore have to set about recording the unemployment status of clients systematically and without delay if they are to have adequate information about the nature of and demand for their facilities and services. Such information would also of course prove of value where adequate proof of increased demand is needed both to justify increased funding and to resist central government constraints on local authorities. Our own referrals exercise has confirmed this.

The Rate Support Grant

11. *Extensive reliance on the social services by vulnerable groups has led to a depletion of resources of all kinds - financial, material and personnel.* The social services, whilst mostly acutely aware of the needs of their users, are unable to meet such needs mainly because of growing financial restraints. Thus in some authorities, like Tower Hamlets, the priority given to maintaining domiciliary services has meant reducing available staffing levels in day centres; in others like Knowsley it has resulted in clear limits to the extent of assistance provided, for example in a refusal to assist those in debt. In all it has encouraged the bare maintenance of conventional practices and has discouraged innovation and change except where such has also happened to cut costs. It has demonstrably led to a failure to meet those growing demands which are related to unemployment.

12. At the annual Social Services Conference in 1984 the Secretary of State for Social Services stated:

> 'More generally I acknowledge that the continuing high level of unemployment places extra pressures on our social services despite the enormous volume of financial underpinning which is being provided to those in need through the social security system.'

In practice however the Government and the DHSS have made little attempt to discover what problems arise from unemployment and have refused to acknowledge that such problems have a significant impact on increased demand for the social services. The measure of the Government's indifference is demonstrated by the increment of 0.05% in the 1984/85 public expenditure figure for the personal social services nationally, to cover unemployment-related expenditure.[13] This works out at £9,940 for each local authority, when the 1984/85 total indicative figure for the personal social services of £2,167 million is divided up. £9,940 would not of course employ a specialist officer to co-ordinate a local authority's response to unemployment, much less meet, for example, the annual growth in welfare rights referrals which in one authority has been in excess of 2,000 a year.

13. The 0.05% growth increment looks distinctly academic not only because it is an underestimate of the increased demand for social services resulting from unemployment, but also because of the decline in the size of the Rate Support Grant. RSG has fallen from 61% of local authorities grant-born-expenditure in 1978/79 to 48.7% in 1985/86, amounting to a loss of revenue of £8 billion in real terms to local government.

Reliance on Social Security and Social Benefits

14. Some commentators assert that the unemployment of the 1980s cannot be compared with that of the '30s because the supporting structure provided by the state is now so much more adequate. In some senses this is true, although the relative disadvantages of the unemployed and particularly the long-term unemployed, are as great as they ever were. The very complexity of the social security system with its increasingly means-tested benefits creates problems which the Government says it is attempting to tackle through the social security reviews. In this survey several problems with benefits were encountered particularly for the physically and mentally handicapped, whose wages in the labour market are potentially among the lowest. Young people are persuaded not to work by their parents, for example, when wages may be as much as £20 a week less than the social security payment. Similarly, mentally ill people in the course of rehabilitation were found to be reluctant to approach Disablement Resettlement Officers for help when such might mean being declared fit for work and then subsequently being unemployed, with benefits replaced by unemployment pay at a lower rate. It is worth noting also, although this was not of concern in this survey, that wives whose husbands are receiving supplementary benefit are deterred from working by the consequent benefit reductions, a fact which just contributes further to 'family unemployment'.

15. Another benefit-related issue which emerged is that in some instances young people in care who are able to find work are pressured not to accept a job offer but remain around the home with their friends, all of them living on supplementary benefit. *This is not an argument for reducing supplementary benefit to an even lower than subsistence level but rather is evidence of the demoralising impact of mass unemployment on communities, where being out of work is the norm.* It gives rise to a youth culture from which the work ethic is gradually and inexorably excluded. Some authorities report that young people have also been turning down jobs because of fear of losing furniture grants from the DHSS. *We believe that, in this instance, social services departments could be of positive assistance by assuring young people of provision of equivalent grants even if a job is accepted.* In all instances it is however not the subsistence level of benefits that is the disincentive to work, but rather the low wages offered, which are not sufficient incentive to depart from the unemployment sub-culture in some areas.

Welfare Rights

16. The complexity of the benefit system, mounting indebtedness, and the information gap, have together combined to increase the welfare rights and financial advisory work of local authorities.[12] In Coventry, for example, welfare rights referrals increased by 46% in the five years between 1978/79 and 1982/83. Similar trends identified throughout the sample highlight this as perhaps *the most significant area of increased demand arising from unemployment.* Critics in both local authority and DHSS circles have argued that this should not be a function of local authorities. In this survey, however, the opposite view was encountered from both managers and practitioners in most authorities. Staff of social services departments in the sample argue that a 'care' element is required alongside provision of 'cash'. Since such a need is not at present part of the role of social security officers, social services departments have an important contribution to make. This care role comprises first, 'advice' on entitlement to benefits and solutions to debt problems, and second 'advocacy' on behalf of claimants and debtors to fuel boards and others.

17. There is also a more pressing rationale for action. Welfare rights and financial advice are necessary to prevent many situations from becoming more serious, time-consuming cases requiring more detailed family intervention and possibly the removal of children into care. Clearly this welfare rights activity is positive, preventative social work and, in the long run, cost-effective. The survey identified increased activity in response to growing demand, but there is widespread anxiety about the capacity of local authorities to meet the need for advice and support at the required level.

Voluntary Organisations and Unemployment

18. This study is not concerned with the employment creation role of voluntary organisations which is largely funded by the MSC. We have, however, noted that the role of voluntary groups in this connection is expanding. We have also noted that the service role of voluntary organisations has been extended in response to unemployment. *Whilst such help is invaluable to individuals who receive it, the provision of support in the areas of our concern is marginal when compared with the investment of staff and money made by local authorities.* Thus the increase in voluntary organisation provision is unlikely to make an impact on a national scale on the problems we have identified. The voluntary organisation is in any event vulnerable because of its dependence on local authority and other public funding which is increasingly under threat.

19. There is nevertheless no doubt that many voluntary and charitable groups have proved their worth as collectors and disseminators of well-researched information on the impact of unemployment, often mounting well-publicised pressure on statutory bodies. They have also been responsible for the introduction of schemes either to help the unemployed cope with their unemployment or become more employable — Mencap's Pathway Scheme to assist handicapped people in finding employment, NACRO's community programme scheme providing employment opportunities for long-term unemployed ex-offenders and MIND's drop-in centres are just three examples among many.

20. Voluntary organisations also often find employment within their organisations for their own clients: Save the Children in Lambeth has found office jobs for children leaving care and the WRVS has found work for the mentally ill in Harrow on its meals on wheels programme. This is a trend which local authorities could follow by making further attempts themselves to employ mentally and physically handicapped people or finding part-time employment for the recovering mentally ill. Such developments are difficult, however, when financial restrictions are enforcing the cutting back of staff and jobs. We are also aware of a recent proposal made by the Association of Directors of Social Services to find jobs for the unemployed in social services departments with joint DHSS and local authority funding. *We think there may be scope for employing some of those marginally employable people who have suffered disproportionately in the recession.*[14]

Local Employers and Unemployed People

21. In the past local authority resources have been supported by the help and good will of local firms willing to take disabled people or children leaving care into their employ. In our sample it is evident that neither the efforts of the local authorities nor of the voluntary organisations are supported in the same way by the attitudes of many local employers or businessmen. *Time and again either indifference or even hostility has been recorded in this survey from local employers whom social services departments have approached.* Whilst this is in many respects understandable during a recession, many staff interviewed feel it belies the many part-time opportunities that could be made available were the will to do so there.

22. The question of the extent to which public, private, local and national firms have a responsibility to the environment in which they operate is a difficult one. Whereas public concern for the physical and ecological environment has often persuaded firms to modify their activities, concern for the social environment has until very recently lacked expression. *We believe there are now excellent grounds for articulating such concern and for encouraging industry and commerce to find work for the disadvantaged.*

Some Broader Issues for the Future

23. Economic predictions are scarcely foolproof but there is little reason to suppose that levels of unemployment will fall in the next few years. Indeed, this year's White Paper on the Government's expenditure plans (Cmnd 9428-1) assumes expenditure on unemployment benefits will continue at a level supporting 3-3½ million unemployed. *The expanding employable age group and the weakness of British manufacturing support the pessimists rather than the optimists and some anticipate a growth in unemployment to over 4 million by the end of the decade.* In this context the approach of the social services to its clients has to be carefully reviewed. Whilst some local communities may actually become so accustomed to unemployment that they develop a correspondingly supportive culture, most will not react so constructively without much encouragement. It is, however, the direction of that encouragement that is so crucial.

24. Two scenarios emerge for the personal social services, with elements of both now visible in current practice. On the one hand unemployment could force the social services into marginal expansion of conventional but perhaps inappropriate facilities. Those who in better times would have been able to work and support themselves would then become doubly disadvantaged, packed into increasingly overcrowded and understaffed centres or dependent for help, support and advice on hopelessly overstretched services. Our research demonstrates that this is now happening in some areas.

25. The alternative, which in some areas now seems inevitable, is the contraction of the social services. This would have even worse consequences. Those whose hold on employment is tenuous would join those who have been mentally ill or are mentally or physically handicapped or who have had the social disadvantage of being brought up in care, forming with them a growing under-class of isolated and alienated people. They would be unable to find work or to obtain any support, help or advice from the personal social services departments. Already this survey has shown that services are contracting in some authorities and others are certainly not able to cope with new demands.

26. These developments pose a question about the role of social services departments. Provision of facilities for the small groups of people who need a particularly sheltered environment is undoubtedly necessary and there is still a serious shortfall in provision for such people. *Clearly, however, for those we have identified as particularly vulnerable to unemployment different solutions are needed as unemployment rises.* Such people need jobs in the first instance, not sheltered environments, so job creation activities are vital. Whilst unemployed, however, such individuals do need structured activities in which the primary goals are self-confidence and employability, with the added target of preventing such people withdrawing from social life. *Without such activities one must anticipate a deterioration in the capacity to cope amongst such individuals and the breakdown of families.* This is a major social policy issue and the question needs to be addressed by central and local government alike: '*Are we prepared to care properly for unemployed people or shall we allow them to slip away from everyday life into deepening isolation and poverty?*'

Conclusion

27. This survey, whilst highlighting some neglected areas of social policy, has uncovered a lack of adequate data in key areas of concern. This should lead to a renewed effort to monitor the impact of unemployment, not only on the personal social services but on other local authority provision, such as education and housing too. Meanwhile we have found and presented clear evidence of changes in the volume and type of demand arising from unemployment of a kind which raises issues to be addressed by both local and central government.

Appendix A
Membership of the Unemployment Research Steering Group

Chairman

David Plank —	Director of Social Services, Hounslow

Members

George Royle —	Director of Social Services, Knowsley (now retired)
Geoff Dunn —	Director of Social Services, Barnsley (now retired)
Bob Hankinson —	Director of Social Services, Sunderland
Malcolm Russell —	Principal Officer, Social Policy, Coventry Social Services Department
Professor Alan Little —	Dean of Social Studies, University of London, Goldsmiths College
Professor Maurice Kogan —	Professor of Government, Brunel University

Secretariat

Peter Westland
Brian Jones
Chris Hume
Susan Balloch

Appendix B
Sample Selection

The sample was not selected randomly. This was considered unnecessary as the study did not involve testing a causal hypothesis and direct comparisons between authorities are not possible due to the variation in data and definitions from one area to another. The only restriction on our choice was the decision to restrict the sample to members of the AMA in view of our special relationship and role. Given these basic premises the aim was to establish a sample which included a balance based on the following criteria:-

(i) ***Geographical Distribution*** — to select authorities, as far as possible, from each of the constituent regions of the Association: Tyne and Wear; Merseyside; Greater Manchester; South Yorkshire; West Yorkshire; West Midlands; Outer London; Inner London.

(ii) *Type of Authority* — There have been various analyses which 'cluster' or 'rank' authorities according to size, socio-economic structure and population. The aim was to avoid selecting a sample of similar authorities e.g. all big cities, or inner-city areas, or traditional heavy engineering areas. To assist in this process we used a range of data including the classification systems of Webber and Craig[1] and Imber[2].

(iii) *Socio-Economic Structure* — To ensure that a particularly distinctive authority was not included in the sample, measures such as numbers of single parents, ethnic origin, and pensioners living alone were compared. In particular a ranked analysis produced by the Department of the Environment[3] was employed.

(iv) ***Unemployment Level*** — Proportion of adult work force unemployed as given by the 1981 census was used to ensure that the sample authorities have at least significant levels of unemployment. Data on duration of unemployment and age structure of the unemployed population were used to ensure that each of the following types of unemployment were represented in the sample:-

Long-term structural unemployment;
Short-term recent unemployment;
Long-term but recent unemployment;
Predominantly youth unemployment;
Predominantly older person's unemployment.

One or more of these types of unemployment can be represented in any one authority.

(v) ***Political Control*** — To ensure that authorities controlled by both major parties were included in the sample.

(vi) ***Population*** — To ensure that a range of population sizes were represented in the sample.

(vii) ***Service Levels*** — Provision in the five service areas selected for detailed study was compared to ensure that the sample includes only those with at least significant levels of provision. For this purpose CIPFA[4] statistics were used.

It was also decided that as well as including authorities identified by the criteria above it would also be of advantage to include an authority with a much lower level of unemployment. There are several advantages in this: firstly, it may demonstrate that the increase in the national level of unemployment is affecting more prosperous areas as well as the inner city; secondly, there may be pockets of unemployment even in prosperous areas causing hardship; and thirdly, it would establish a 'marker' against which the severity of problems in inner areas could be contrasted.

Appendix C
Economic Profiles

Included in this Appendix are brief economic profiles of the eight metropolitan authority areas selected for this unemployment research. These outline the way in which unemployment has developed in these authorities during the post-war period. They also given details of other related features such as demographic changes, movements of industry and commerce, and changing patterns in social life. These profiles provide information which is not given in detail in the main text, but which is of course very relevant to the problems central to this study.

Coventry

Rebuilt after the ferocious bombing of World War II, Coventry in the West Midlands enjoyed a period of unrivalled prosperity and full employment until the end of the 1960s. Aerospace, engineering and the motor vehicle industries all contributed to an expanding manufacturing sector in which over half the population was employed. This relatively narrow manufacturing base showed first signs of vulnerability to recession in the late 1960s and became particularly hard-pressed after the 1974 oil crisis. As a result the work-force was faced for the first time in memory with an extended period of increasing unemployment.

The city's population had grown rapidly up to this point and was still dominated by young working people with growing families. Between 1971 and 1981, however, the population of Coventry showed signs of both decline and age. In that decade a fall in

Table 1 — Coventry Population in 1971-1991 (Numbers and Percentages)

	Persons Aged 0-4		Persons Aged 5-9		Persons Aged 10-17		Persons Aged 18-64		Persons Aged 65-74		Persons Aged 75 +		All Ages	
Census Year	No	%	No	%	No	%	No	%	No	%	No	%	No	%
1971	30,010	8.9	30,469	9.0	41,248	12.3	200,737	59.6	22,850	6.8	11,406	3.4	336,720	100
1981	19,164	6.2	20,872	6.7	42,937	13.8	185,796	59.9	27,022	8.7	14,425	4.7	310,216	100
1991	23.234	7.6	20,705	6.8	29,610	9.7	181,476	59.8	28,662	9.4	20,333	6.7	303,720	100

population of 8% was recorded with a continuing, though slower, decline anticipated in the 1980s. As in other situations, the elderly in the population expanded rapidly, both in absolute and relative terms, whilst the numbers of young children fell. Teenagers, however, increased in number as a result of the high birth rate amongst the population in the early 1960s. Today trends are changing, with the under-fives again on the increase and the teenage population in decline.

Post-war expansion in Coventry attracted many from overseas — both from India (3.8% of the population in 1981) and the West Indies (0.6% in 1981); many also came from Ireland and various parts of Europe. Coventry has not, however, suffered from the racial violence experienced in other areas. It has been suggested that this may be because immigrants to Coventry have comprised only part of a large expansion in population rather than replacements to long established communities. Today approximately 19.5% of Coventry's population consists of those households where the head was born in the New Commonwealth or Pakistan; slightly over one third of these are children under 16.

In 1973 unemployment in Coventry affected only 2.3% of the workforce. After a slow, if steady, rise in the 1970s it rose dramatically in 1981 and in January 1985 rests at 18.4%, well above the national level. For men unemployment seems to be fairly evenly spready across the age groups but for women is concentrated amongst the young, with over half unemployed women under 25. About 75% of the unemployed have been out of work for more than six months and 50% for over a year. Youth unemployment is of particular concern; an analysis of the 16 year-old school leavers in 1983 showed only 14% in work by the end of that year with 38% on YTS, 6% unemployed and 38% in full-time education.

Although the unemployment rate has more than trebled since the 1970s its incidence has varied across the city, ranging by ward from 9.5% to 36.5% with the highest levels in the east. This is because the Coventry economy is not made up of several local economies, but is rather a relatively large and well integrated economy stretching beyond the city even into parts of Warwickshire. As such it is felt that economic regeneration needs to be viewed from a city-wide or sub-regional perspective. Nevertheless it remains the case that wards with especially high levels of unemployment and deprivation are also likely to contain a higher than average number of people for whom local work is a necessity. For those without private transport or with dependent children or relatives, local work opportunities are of prime importance.

The London Boroughs

Three London boroughs have participated in this survey — Harrow, Lambeth and Tower Hamlets. Of these Harrow has a lower index of deprivation and unemployment, and in contrast to the other two inner-city areas which, on OPCS indicators, encompass some of the poorest and most troubled areas of the metropolis. Yet important parallels also exist between these three which deserve some comment.

Firstly, they all contain declining populations characterised by a high, if not increasing, percentage of elderly people. Population decline is generally brought about by a fall in fertility and by out-migration of more mobile individuals usually in skilled employment. In the latter case, those left behind are likely to be unskilled and vulnerable to unemployment, or immobile and dependent because of handicap or age. In either instance, these groups encompass large numbers requiring help from the social services. Secondly, the three boroughs all have concentrations of ethnic minorities: Asians in Harrow, West Indians in Lambeth and Asians, especially Bangladeshis, in Tower Hamlets. These minorities tend to be living in more deprived surroundings and experiencing more severe unemployment than their white neighbours. These people are the first to leave employment and the last to re-enter during times of recession and are disproportionately affected by their large numbers of young people, for many of whom employment has ceased to be a reality.Thirdly, Harrow, Lambeth and Tower Hamlets are all closely linked economically with other London boroughs. Their populations may travel to work over considerable distances and are quickly affected by a rise or fall in employment elsewhere. In all three, however, the decline of local employment prospects has presented a particularly serious situation for those unable to afford the high cost of travel or those with dependent children or relatives who rely on local work.

Finally, it is important to note that the true extent of unemployment in these areas is hard to define. For the purposes of this survey, the figures used have been supplied by the planning departments of the authorities concerned, mainly on the basis of 1981 census and GLC estimates. The Greater London unemployment rate is calculated by the London Voluntary Service Council using first the numbers of registered unemployed summarised on a borough basis through the MSC and relating these to secondly the level of economically active population resident in each London borough at 1984 from an interpolation of projections of the 1981 census figures provided by the GLC.

These figures present a more detailed estimate than can Department of Employment figures, based as they have been since 1982 on benefit claimants; they are also more useful than local Department of Employment figures which are based on travel to work areas devised some time ago as an economic indicator of surplus labour and which do not coincide with either wards or borough or constituency boundaries. The inner London consultative employment group, a body on which the GLC, inner boroughs, chambers of commerce and trade unions are represented has argued recently that Whitehall statistics effectively disguised the extent of London's unemployment and allow the problem to be swamped by the relative prosperity of the south-east region.

Harrow

Harrow is an outer-London borough in pleasant green belt surroundings, mainly characterised today by light industries and services. Its population has declined slowly since the 1950s and at the 1981 census stood at 196,159 of whom about 97,000 are economically active. Between 1971 and 1981 the number of children in Harrow under 9 years fell by 21% due to the sharp decline in the birth rate, but an increase of 12% in the 10 to 19 age group has resulted in more school-age children and more school leavers than in the 1970s. Consequently Harrow's labour force will show a slight increase in the 1980s to approximately 99,000 in 1991. Other features of population change in the last census period include a decrease of 23% in the 50 to 64 age group, attributed to outward migration from Harrow and an increase of 27.8% in the frail elderly.

The population in households with the head of the household

born in the New Commonwealth or Pakistan has increased from 12,000 in 1971 to 29,761 in 1981, or 15% of 1981 total population. Their age structure is significantly different from the rest of the population, with only 4% over pensionable age and 28.3% under 16. The distribution of this population throughout Harrow has been changing recently, with the largest decreases occurring in the areas around Harrow and Wealdstone town centres and the main increases in Pinner, Hatch End and Ridgeway in new housing developments. There is a wide variation in the distribution of the New Commonwealth and Pakistani population throughout the borough, with the highest concentrations around Wealdstone town centre, Roxeth Ward and the Kenton/Burnt Oak areas with the wards in the north and north west below 10%.

Harrow's changing employment structure has shown a typical decline of manufacturing employment and a growth of service sector jobs. Manufacturing employment fell from 14,350 in 1971 to under 12,000 in 1978 but this was offset by the growth in office and other non-manual opportunities. In 1971/81, for example, although 18 firms closed down in Harrow, another 17 opened. Economic change and the inevitable mismatch of skills has still, however, created unemployment. As the general economic situation worsened, the total numbers of registered unemployed in Harrow rose from 5,613 in April 1982 to 6,254 or 6.4% in January 1985, a rate still far below that for Lambeth and Tower Hamlets.

Amongst the unemployed, the numbers of young people have been rising as the following table indicates.

Table 2 — Young People Unemployed In Harrow

	Under 18s	Aged 18	Aged 19+	Total
October 1982	247	87	324	658
August 1983	69	64	441	574
August 1984	80	117	468	665

Harrow's Policy and Resources Committee has recorded the disproportionate impact that they believe unemployment has had on the young and has illustrated this with information on notified vacancies and numbers unemployed between 1979 and 1982.

Table 3 — Impact of Unemployment in Harrow on Young People

	Registered Adult Unemployed	Notified Vacancies	16–19 Unemployed	Notified Vacancies
1979	2,074	761	207	167
1980	2,512	445	387	47
1981	4,145	328	507	12

Whilst these vacancies were mainly in office work, most of the unemployed were relatively unskilled.

Lambeth

The South London Borough of Lambeth illustrates the sad case of inner-city decline. Its shrinking population and decreasing employment opportunities contrast with the stable proportion of elderly and the growing numbers of one-parent families. Between 1971 and 1981 the population fell by 20%, from 307,000 to 246,000; this fall was most marked amongst children under 5 (42%) and school-age children (32%). Correspondingly, the numbers of the economically active fell from 160,000 to 130,000.

The ethnic composition of the population has also been changing, with a drop in the numbers born in the Caribbean being balanced by a rise in those born in Africa, Sri Lanka and the Far East. In 1981, Lambeth's ethnic minorities averaged 23% of the population and, whilst being widely spread throughout the borough were particularly concentrated in Herne Hill (Area 3), Brixton (Area 5) and Streatham (Area 7).

As population declined between 1971 and 1981, so the unemployment rate doubled, from a borough average of 6% to 13%. Since then unemployment has continued to rise. Figures supplied by Lambeth's Economic Activity and Employment Committee record total unemployment increasing by 189% between 1979 and 1983; in 1979 there were four people unemployed for every notified vacancy, but by June 1983 this number had risen to 45:. Within this period female unemployment rose faster than male (up 240% compared with 172%), youth unemployment rose by 165% and long-term unemployment by a shocking 306%.

Black unemployment also rose rapidly but here the figures are less exact. Over the 1981/82 period black unemployment was rising faster than that of whites. By March 1982, blacks formed 8% of all unemployed in London and 17% of all unemployed in Lambeth with 63% of these registered in Brixton. Since then the system of compiling unemployment statistics has not included information on the ethnic origin of benefit claimants, although discussions on collecting information on the ethnic origin of the unemployed are currently in progress with the Department of Employment. The latest available figure was for August 1982 when there were 3,773 unemployed black people in the Borough (17%). Assuming the population remains similar in 1984 that figure should now stand at 4,360.

Because of the impact of unemployment in Lambeth, and above all the effect on black youth, there is again a real fear of violence. Lambeth became the focus of national attention in the summer of 1981 when riots in Brixton set the streets alight. These had marked the end of a decade in which there had been a 41% loss of manufacturing jobs and a 55% decline in construction work. An increase in commercial and service work was of little help to the many unqualified and unskilled in search of local work. Three years ago, in his subsequent inquiry into the riots, Lord Scarman commented on the desperate need to improve job opportunities for black people and in particular for the young. On returning to the scene he has again recently reiterated this need in the light of current unemployment trends. He has also emphasised how the closure of services such as youth clubs, which might well result from rate capping, could easily create the spark to set the streets alight again.

The most recent evidence on unemployment supports these fears. Since March 1983 unemployment has risen by 7.8%, with young people, women and blacks still the hardest hit. Lambeth's unemployment rate is now the third highest of all London boroughs, remains significantly above the regional and national averages and is even higher than the rates for the so-called 'depressed' areas. The latest figures have recorded a total of 24,891 unemployed against 451 notified vacancies.

Table 4 — Unemployment Rates: March 1983 — March 1984

Area	Male		Female		Total	
	1983	1984	1982	1984	1983	1984
Lambeth	23.3%	24.0%	12.2%	13.7%	18.5%	19.6%
GLC	12.0%	11.9%	6.4%	7.2%	9.7%	10.0%
South East	12.5%	11.6%	6.4%	7.1%	10.0%	9.7%
UK	16.8%	15.7%	9.0%	9.5%	13.6%	13.2%
GB	16.6%	15.4%	8.9%	9.4%	13.5%	13.0%

Tower Hamlets

Like other long established inner-city areas, Tower Hamlets has been progressively losing its population throughout this century, with a decline from 600,000 in 1900 to 144,500 in 1982, including a recorded loss of 14% over the last inter-census decade. The remaining population now exhibits a higher dependency rate than average, with 17% of pensioners and 21% of children; unusually, the percentage of pensioners in the population is now static, but that of young children is rising. Even if the economically active population were fully employed, it would still have to support a greater proportion of dependants than other Londoners.

Tower Hamlets has the ninth highest proportion of ethnic minorities amongst all district authorities in the country with the largest group being Bangladeshi (about 10% of the household population). This population is, in contrast to other sectors, growing at a relatively rapid rate so that it now accounts for about 40% of all the borough's births. Census statistics show clearly that the ethnic minority households live in greater poverty than do other residents and are concentrated in the relatively deprived areas of Spitalfields, St Mary's and St Katharine's. Recent research has indicated much racial tension and harassment in the borough.

Tower Hamlets has always been characterised by manual labour, with cargo handling, storage and distribution the major activities around the docks; and clothing, furniture and leather goods firms dominating the west of the borough. Since it is these occupations, in contrast to the services, that have been hardest hit by unemployment, it is not surprising to find a much higher level of unemployment concentrated in Tower Hamlets than is found in London as a whole.

The 1981 Census recorded unemployment as 16% or 10,800 of the economically active population. The incidence was far greater for men than women (19% and 11% respectively), very high for teenagers, with 22% of 16-19 year-olds without employment, and was concentrated in particular in certain unemployment black spots such as Spitalfields, St Mary's, St Dunstan's, Limehouse and Blackwall.

Since the census the recession has hit harder, with unemployment rising to an average of 22% and about 29% of economically active men. A recent question in the House of Commons on London's dockland boroughs elicited the information that in May 1984 11,395 were unemployed in Tower Hamlets of which nearly one third were under 25. Nearly half had been unemployed for over a year.

Knowsley

Knowsley Borough is one of five districts which together constitute the metropolitan county of Merseyside. It came into existence in April 1974 to encompass the towns of Kirkby, Huyton, Prescot, Whiston and Halewood. Two-thirds of the borough is green-belt land, but the rest encompasses three huge industrial complexes to which much of Liverpool's original population moved in the 1950s and 1960s for rehousing and employment. The development of such 'outer estates', spawned initially by slum clearance in inner-city areas, occurred in several parts of the country, but today the energy and vitality that this expressed has been dissipated by factory closures and hyper-unemployment.

On the basis of 1971 Census data cluster analysis, Knowsley appeared an extreme, if not unique, authority, with 9.6% of its population under five years old and 69.5% of all households in public housing. Ten years later, in comparison with all 36 metropolitan districts, Knowsley still had a high birth rate giving it one of the highest proportions of under-24 year-olds and the highest proportion of council housing. Basically, Knowsley remains at the extreme of all the metropolitan districts on measures of social deprivation, with a youthful and impoverished population more than usually dependent on public support.

Between 1971 and 1981 the Borough's population fell overall by

11% to 172,991. From 1974 to 1981, the percentage of 5-14 year-olds fell by about one third and the numbers of children under 4 by 10%. Though there was only a small increase in the 65-74 year-olds, there was a 20% increase in the frail elderly. The council forecasts a continued increase in the over-75s, but also, in line with national trends, a renewed increase in the number of under-4s. Given that Knowsley has the highest proportion of one-parent households amongst the metropolitan districts, many of these children must be anticipated in one-parent families, with the mothers inevitably young, unemployed and dependent on social security.

Knowsley also has the highest proportion of economically active men and women seeking work and within this figure an alarmingly high proportion of young people. As a corollorary, the proportion of residents in work is very low, broadly increasing the dependence of more people on those left in work. The background to this unemployment is the decline of Merseyside, which has witnessed the closures of many major factories, including Dunlop, Tate & Lyle, Courtaulds, Hygena, Metal Box and Meccano. In 1981, unemployment in Knowsley stood at 22%. It peaked in January 1984 at 26.4%. The figures for September 1984 record 20,827 (15,342 men and 5,485 women) or 25.7% of the working population out of work.

A debate on youth unemployment in the House of Commons early this year illustrated this in detail. It was noted that Knowsley had the highest youth unemployment in Britain, with 85% of school leavers in Knowsley North either unemployed or on YTS. In Kirkby, where the industrial estates are rapidly becoming deserted, 5,949 men were chasing 7 jobs, with 1,764 unemployed women and 252 unemployed school leavers.

Kirkby has provided a focus in a recent survey analysing the decline of four 'outer estates' built on the fringes of cities in the 1950s and 1960s. Typically unemployment has reduced the community to an existence at little more than subsistence level; little cash is circulating, most households are dependent on housing benefit, fuel debts are mounting and local shops are in decline. With nobody commuting into the area, no influx of income can alleviate the situation, and to impoverishment is added an isolation bedevilled by both the lack of private transport and inadequate public services. In sum, communities like that of Kirkby are worse off than many inner-city areas, yet have to survive with little of the government aid that the latter may receive.

Bradford

In many respects Bradford is perhaps the most complete example of a city suffering the social and economic problems of the 1980s. It manifests: economic decline; unemployment; urban decline; depreciating housing stock and a large underprivileged ethnic grouping, all in one city and in significant measured amounts.

At the last census (1981)[1] Bradford was ranked 28th local authority in England out of 365 in terms of overcrowding, 34th ranked in terms of numbers of single parents and 53rd ranked in terms of unemployment. These rankings will undoubtedly have worsened as Bradford's economic decline has become increasingly spectacular.

In common with a handful of other big cities in England, Bradford is suffering at the hands of the decline of its one big industry which brought the city to prominence in the last century — in Bradford's case the industry in question is textiles.

> 'In ten years the district has moved from full employment, a superficially healthy-looking economy and relative prosperity for virtually everyone to massive factory closures, 37,000 unemployed, 57,000 people on supplementary benefit — and for thousands the apparent end of their hopes of a decent career, income and lifestyle'. (City of Bradford, *The Changing Face of Bradford*, 1984).

The Governments official unemployment figure for Bradford in May 1984 was 29,000. In reality if unemployment figures were calculated in the same way as prior to October 1982 — that is all those signing on available for work — another 3,000 would be added to this total to make 32,000. An unemployment rate of over 15%. These figures are a major increase on the figures for the early 1970s, the official number of people unemployed in 1974 was 5,000. The causes of the vast increase in unemployment on the one hand are due to the recession of the past 5 years, but also due to the particular decline of Bradford's predominantly manufacturing industrial base in the face of overseas competition and declining markets. Manufacturing industry has declined far more than service industries in recent years and this has disproportionately affected towns like Bradford which have traditionally had large manufacturing sectors. In 1961 61% of Bradford's workforce were employed in manufacturing. Although growth in jobs in the service sector in Bradford actually was higher than the national average creating 26,000 new jobs, the decline in manufacturing jobs in the same period was 54,000. A net decline of 28,000. 45,000 of the jobs lost in manufacturing were in textiles alone. Bradford lost nearly a quarter of its jobs in the twenty years to 1981.

It is impossible to describe whether Bradford is poorer now than in the early 1970s before the recession. But the district's economic decline has undoubtedly affected some groups much more than others, particularly the young, the unskilled and black people. The inequalities which are always present in society have been deepened by the progress of change, to the point where they can now be measured virtually area by areas.

Particular groups are hardest hit by unemployment:-

(i) The young — in 1979 86% of school leavers in Bradford found work, in 1984 it was only 35%;

(ii) Ethnic minorities — although black people comprise 10% of the work-force as many as 25% are estimated as being unemployed. This means that young black people are doubly disadvantaged;

(iii) Less skilled — many of the jobs lost over the last decade have been unskilled e.g. in September 1982 8,000 people registered at job centres seeking general labouring work. Just 14 suitable vacancies have been notified in the previous three months;

(iv) Geography — unemployment is much higher in two particular areas of the city: the inner areas and outer council estates. Unemployment is having a devastating effect in these areas.

In April 1984, 12,500 people in Bradford had been out of work for over a year, and of these 7,000 had been out of work for over two years.

Given this background of economic decline and change, there is a notable decline in income and lifestyle of many families.

> 'What does seem new is that poverty is no longer confined to individuals and small pockets in the districts. It affecting whole communities, and affecting them selectively. Parts of the district are becoming virtually 'poverty zones' with a few working people, low

incomes and many dependants — while other parts are remaining relatively prosperous.' (City of Bradford, *Bradford in Figures*, 1984).

In some of the large council estates unemployment can be approaching 50% whereas in the more prosperous areas it can be as low as 5%. The average working person in a poorer area is supporting two other people; in the more prosperous areas only one. This division into richer and poorer areas means that whole areas can no longer support facilities which other areas take for granted and which rely more and more on the public sector. The local authority in particular highlights the lack of facilities and depreciation of the large council estates, where health is affected by declining access to nutritious food and social facilities, the environment is depreciating and access to a better environment is reduced as car ownership declines.

A significant factor in Bradford is the size of the ethnic minority group within the population and any findings cannot ignore this phenomenon. Bradford is a city of many races and cultures but the most significant minority grouping is of an Asian origin. The 1981 census shows that 1 in 10 Bradfordians were born outside the UK; a further 1 in 20 were born in the UK but had parents born outside the UK. This meant that out of the total population of Bradford roughly 1 in 7 i.e. 72,000 lived in households where the head of household was born outside the UK, of whom 53,000 were from the New Commonwealth. The Asian population alone comprises 65% of the total (immigrant) community.

Sunderland

Sunderland has many similarities to Bradford. It is a town which is suffering from economic decline as a result of the decline of a traditional industrial base established in the last century. The main difference is that the economic decline is an older phenomenon in Sunderland and unemployment has existed for much longer. Sunderland however does not manifest outward signs of decline and depression to the same degree as Bradford, particularly in its inner areas.

There is no question that the economic decline has been as severe in Sunderland. The source of this decline is the erosion of Sunderland's two primary industries: shipbuilding and coal-mining. Hitherto these two industries alone employed the majority of working people in Sunderland. Their decline over the last 20 to 30 years, preceding the recession of the last years, has been dramatic and affected whole communities. There has remained until recent years an over-dependence throughout the whole economy on manufacturing industry, leading to a preponderence of unskilled and semi-skilled labour and few job opportunities for young people. This has meant that the local economy has been slow to recover from both the recession and the long-term decline in the heavy industries resulting from national and international demand.

> 'Unemployment is Sunderland's most serious and pervasive problem. There is hardly an aspect of life in the town which is not affected by it, of a service of the authority which does not bear additional problems because of it.' (Borough of Sunderland, Programme Planning Department, *Borough Profile*).

Even in 1980 one in seven of the total work-force were unemployed; 16% of men and 10.5% of women. This has now risen to an unemployment rate of 21.2% overall or 29,514. The pattern of unemployment is localised with some of the older inner parts e.g. Southwick having experienced unemployment for a number of years. These areas have traditionally contained those people who work in either coal-mining or shipbuilding. In Southwick, which is situated immediately adjacent to the ship-yards, the unemployment rate is 22.2% and in some smaller areas within the ward it is 50%; 30% of the population work in manufacturing industry and 83.1% are described as either skilled manual, partly skilled or unskilled. The other areas were unemployment is disproportionately concentrated are the outlying council estates where it is a much more recent phenomenon.

Although unemployment is disproportionately high in both types of area — older inner areas and outer estates — the people in the older inner areas appear to be coping far better than those on the outer estates. Social workers and others see two reasons for this: firstly unemployment has been around for much longer in these older areas and people have learnt to 'put on a brave face'; secondly there is a greater sense of community and less isolation in the older areas.

This second phenomenon is largely peculiar to Sunderland and results from the fact that the older parts of Sunderland are primarily a collection of 'villages' or distinct established communities. Despite the extreme levels of unemployment in these villages, such as Southwick, there is no prevailing atmosphere of gloom and despondency and the key seems to be the strength of community spirit. These villages have their own shopping centre and place of gathering, a large number of pubs and community groups, therefore personal contact is frequent. In contrast on the outlying estates there is little sense of community, few pubs and meeting points and a greater propensity to social isolation therefore people find little help with their problems.

Population decline has not been significant in Sunderland as a whole. The net decline between 1971 and 1981 was 1,656 or 0.6%; this is not very significant compared to other metropolitan authorities. The primary reason why population decline is not very significant is the development of Washington New Town which has shown a marked increase in population. If this disaggregation is also focused on the inner areas of Sunderland town itself a marked decline in population is revealed. Within this trend the older inner areas have seen increasing concentration of elderly people. High fertility has been a feature of Washington New Town and the outer estates, maintaining a youthful population for the borough as a whole.

Manchester

Manchester is qualitatively and quantitatively different from the other authorities in the sample as it is by far the largest single city. In contrast to the other large cities its industry is not dominated by one or more traditional heavy industry. Nevertheless, the unemployment rate has shown a marked increase in recent years and it is one of the country's major unemployment black spots.

Table 5 — Unemployment Rates in Manchester

		Percent		
	Number	**Males**	**Females**	**Total**
Great Britain	3,270,853	16.3	10.1	13.7
Manchester TTWA	112,284	18.2	9.8	14.7
City of Manchester	44,764	29.6	14.7	23.6

Source: City of Manchester, Planning Department, Unemployment and Vacancies, January 1985.

In April 1984 21.1% of all unemployed social security claimants had been unemployed for between 1 and 2 years; 13.1% between 2 and 3 years and 17% for over 3 years.

The major source of unemployment in Manchester has been a long-term decline in manufacturing, in particular medium-scale engineering which was widespread throughout the city. More recently this has been exacerbated by declining service sector employment. The financial impact unemployment has had on the population figures can be shown by the number of people in Manchester dependent on supplementary benefit.

According to the City of Manchester Planning Department, 75,664 people were receiving supplementary benefit in the city in February 1983. (City of Manchester, Planning Department, *Economic Indicators*.)

Table 6 — Families with Children and Claiming Supplementary Benefit in Manchester

Year	Families in Manchester
November 1979	15,000
December 1980	19,000
December 1981	25,000
December 1982	27,000

Source: **Hansard**; 23 July 1984.

Unemployment is heaviest amongst unskilled and semi-skilled workers and it is in this sector where vacancies are lowest. Other groups suffering the heaviest unemployment are young people under the age of 25. For example, in January 1984, 18% of claimants were under 18 and nearly 22% between 20 and 24. The other group disproportionately represented amongst the unemployed in Manchester are ethnic minority groups. Between February 1980 and August 1982 registered unemployment amongst ethnic groups rose from 1,307 to 3,136, 6.8% of the total unemployment in Manchester, which is not significantly greater than the proportion of the total population of ethnic minority origin. However, unemployment appears to be far more significant amongst the West Indian community than amongst other ethnic groups.

Manchester City Council has responded positively to the unemployment crisis in the city. An internal briefing document 'Local Government and the Unemployment' identifies the following as the main effects of unemployment:-

— financial pressures;
— family stress caused by more intensive relationships;
— loss of social networks and withdrawal into the home;
— loss of self-confidence;
— lack of access to creative activity;
— difficulties in structuring time.

In response to these problems, and within their limited powers, the city council has developed a number of initiatives ranging from welfare rights campaigns to reduced or nil charges to unemployed people for leisure facilities. Manchester has also encouraged the development of drop-in centres for the unemployed, and has created an Economic Development Unit concentrating on the needs of the unemployed.

APPENDIX D
Some Comments on Unemployment and Child Abuse

1. Early on in this research the likelihood of a link between unemployment and non-accidental injury to children seemed worth investigating. Since then the publication by the NSPCC of *Trends in Child Abuse* has reported a marked increase in trends of children injured by their parents over the last six years in areas where the NSPCC has special units.[1] Although serious and fatal injuries were found to have declined, less serious injuries were estimated to have increased by 47%. Most significantly the report argued that one of the factors associated with this upward trend was rising unemployment and consequential family stress.

2. The proportion of unemployed fathers of abused children showed an increase from 35% in 1977 to 58.2% in 1982, with the ratio of employed to unemployed among fathers showing a complete reversal during the study period. Although very few of the mothers of abused children are economically active, unemployment was shown to have spread amongst them too, with 17.6% of the mothers employed in 1977 but only 12.6% by 1981. At the same time, the percentage of the abused children's families in receipt of supplementary benefit had risen to nearly two-thirds by 1982. Some of the report's findings are summarised below.

3. Findings from the AMA survey confirmed an upward trend in new registrations of children at risk in all authorities between 1979 and 1982.

Table 1 — Employment Characteristics of Parents of Abused Children by Year

Year	Mothers		Fathers		Supplementary Benefit
	Employed*	Unemployed	Employed*	Unemployed	Recipients
1977	123 (17.6)	494 (70.7)	331 (53.4)	217 (35.0)	337 (46.6)
1978	111 (15.0)	592 (80.2)	350 (56.4)	219 (35.3)	301 (40.2)
1979	104 (15.5)	555 (82.7)	330 (57.2)	230 (39.9)	303 (42.6)
1980	122 (15.6)	601 (76.7)	313 (47.1)	257 (38.7)	367 (45.0)
1981	109 (12.6)	704 (81.2)	227 (38.7)	371 (51.8)	514 (57.2)
1982	98 (12.9)	622 (81.8)	226 (36.9)	365 (58.2)	483 (61.7)

* Percentages relate to the different numbers of mothers and fathers in the sample when parental situation is adjusted for.

Table 2 — New Registrations of Children at Risk

	1978/79	1979/80	1980/81	1981/82	1982/83
Coventry	96	104	93	99	127
Lambeth	87	43	71	98	116
Harrow	—	25	24	35	30
Tower Hamlets	27	44	39	65	87
Manchester	108 ('78)	97 ('79)	145 ('80)	128 ('81)	150 ('82)
Sunderland	33	29	30	24	55
Bradford	—	129 ('79)	127 ('80)	233 ('81)	215 ('82)
Knowsley	24	42	45	30	35

Specific illustration of this trend has been provided by Coventry. Here the figures for the number of new registrations of children at risk between 1978-79 and 1982-83 showed an increase of 32%. Figures from the NSPCC special unit in Coventry also showed a significant increase in the number of referrals from 28 in 1978 to 62 in 1983. (Table 3) Throughout the period the incidence of unemployment amongst parents of abused children remained high; in 1978, 58% of fathers and 86% of mothers were unemployed. By 1983 these figures had risen steadily to 65% of fathers and 92% of mothers. It has to be noted, however, that these figures are for the total number of children registered not just for those non-accidentally injured. Since a 1980 DHSS circular widened the criteria for registration from cases of physical injury and non-organic failure to thrive to include cases of neglect, emotional or sexual

Table 3 — The Effects of Unemployment — from the NSPCC Special Unit, Coventry

Codes: NP: Natural parents
NMA: Natural Mother Alone
NFA: Natural Father Alone
NM/FS: Natural Mother and Father Substitute
NF/MS: Natural Father and Mother Substitute

YEAR	2NP	NMA	NFA	NM/FS	NF/MS	TOTAL	Unemployed Mother/Father		Employed Mother/Father		Unemployed Father %	Unemployed Mother %
1975	2	—	—	2	—	7	6	3	1	4	43	86
1976	10	9	—	9	1	29	28	11	1	9	55	97
1977	9	7	3	10	—	29	26	16	—	7	70	100
1978	18	2	4	4	—	28	24	15	4	11	58	86
1979	16	6	2	5	—	29	21	6	6	17	26	78
1980	15	4	1	8	—	28	27	12	—	11	52	100
1981	20	18	3	11	3	55	44	21	6	14	66	88
1982	16	4	1	7	2	30	28	14	2	12	54	93
1983	23	10	3	22	4	62	55	20	5	11	65	92
TOTAL	132	60	17	78	10	297	259	118	25	96		

abuse, overall registrations were almost bound to increase in 1981. This change makes it very difficult to draw any conclusions about increases in registrations between 1979 and 1983. Information on non-accidental injury cases only would have been more useful, but this was not available.

4. Figures provided by three authorities, Manchester, Bradford and Sunderland, also suggest a recent downward turn in this trend. In Manchester, new registrations dropped from 150 in 1982 to 127 in 1983; in Bradford they fell from 215 in 1982 to 111 in 1983 and in Sunderland from 55 in 1982-83 to 45 in 1984. In Manchester and Bradford social workers and their officers have explained this as the result of a relaxation of attitudes. In the light of previous publicity and, in Bradford's case, a child's death, social workers have felt obliged to report trivial instances and use registration as a general 'safety net'. This has now ceased, hence, it was argued, the drop in registration. In Bradford it was also suggested that violence was being spotted sooner and social work intervention was occurring at an earlier stage before registration became necessary. In Sunderland, however, the drop in new registrations was not considered to be particularly significant, but to be related to changes in record-keeping. This shows with what caution such figures need to be treated. Although the upward trend in new registrations between 1979 and 1982 might be related to rising unemployment, further, more detailed research is necessary to establish the specific ramifications of this hypothesis and to explore the assumptions involved. This was beyond the scope of this study.

5. Scepticism was also encountered amongst some officers on the impact of unemployment on child abuse. In Manchester for example it was reported that an NSPCC analysis had found little or no evidence, amongst those whose children were placed on its register, of unemployment exerting any greater collective impact, despite the increase in the numbers of unemployed and the families thus affected.

6. Here then is an area of controversy which as yet must go unresolved. It is still our belief, however, that unemployment has a most serious effect on the family life in the stresses caused and the children thus put at risk. In Bradford, for example, officers reported that some Asian families, now especially hard hit by unemployment, were under great stress. Their traditional emphasis on the importance of the male breadwinner and his support of both his family and the local community has left unemployed fathers with severe guilt feelings and driven mothers towards suicide. This may be one cause behind the child abuse said to exist in some Asian communities. Whilst accepting that many factors contribute to child abuse, it is hard to doubt that children are put at risk when the stresses of unemployment and poverty are added to the other strains of family life. Given that, as a direct result of unemployment, some 4 million children are now living in poverty[2], there must be *a serious fear of increasing rather than declining levels of child abuse throughout the rest of the 1980s.*

REFERENCES

INTRODUCTION

1. House of Commons — *Hansard*, Parliamentary Written Answers, *15 February 1984*, HMSO

CHAPTER ONE

1. Hawkins, K — *Unemployment*, Pelican, 1984
2. Popay, J — 'Unemployment and the Family' *Unemployment Alliance Briefing Paper No. 4* 1984
3. City of Bradford — *The Changing Face of Bradford: District Trends 1984*, City of Bradford Metropolitan District, 1984
4. Sinfield, A — *What Unemployment Means*, Martin Robinson, 1981
5. Hill, M et al — *Men Out of Work*, CVP, 1973
6. Taylor, S — 'De-industrialisation and Unemployment in the West Midlands', in Crick B (Ed) *Unemployment*, Methuen, 1981
7. Sinfield, A — Op cit, 1981
8. Centre for Environmental Studies — *The Outer Estates*, CES, 1984
9. Smith, D J — *The Facts of Racial Disadvantage: A National Survey*, PEP Report 560, 1976
10. Brown, C — *Black and White Britain: The Third PSI Survey*, Heinemann Educational Books, 1984
11. Taylor, M — *Growing up Without Work*, European Centre for Work and Society, Studies and Documents 4, 1983
12. City of Bradford — Op cit, 1984

13. Anwar, M — *Young People in the Job Market — A Survey*, Commission for Racial Equality, 1982

14. Amsden, A — *The Economics of Women and Work*, Penguin 1980

15. H.M. Government — *Royal Commission on the Distribution of Income and Wealth*, Volume 6, HMSO, Cmnd 7175, 1978

16. Joshi, H — 'Women's Participation in Paid Work. A Regression Analysis of the Women and Unemployment Survey', *Departmentof Employment Research Paper*, 1984

17. Bradshaw, J, Cooke, K and Godfrey, C — 'The Impact of Unemployment on the Living Standards of Families', *Journal of Social Policy 12.4*, pp 438-452, October 1983

18. The Economist — 5 November 1983

19. House of Commons Debate — *Hansard*, Debate on Unemployment 22 February 1984

20. Jones, P — 'Effects of Rising Unemployment on School Leavers', *Department of Employment Gazette*, January 1983

21. House of Commons Debate — *Hansard*, 22 February 1984, column 858, HMSO

22. Sinfield, A — Op cit, 1981

23. For a useful resumé of these other studies see Oliver, C. 'Older Workers and Unemployment', *Unemployment Alliance Briefing Paper No 3*, April 1982

24. Parker, S R — *Older Workers and Retirement*, OPCS, 1980

25. Department of Employment — *Department of Employment Gazette*, February 1985

26. Maglan S and Davies B — 'The Disadvantages of the Unemployed', in the *Department of Employment Gazette*, August 1980

27. Bradshaw, J, Cooke, K and Godfrey, C — Op cit, 1983

28. Walker, A — *Unqualified and Underemployed: Handicapped Young People in the Labour Market*. National Children's Bureau, 1982

29. Fagin, L — *Unemployment and Health in Families, Case Studies Based on Family Interviews*, DHSS, 1981

30. Platt, S — 'Unemployment and Attempted Suicide in Edinburgh 1968-1982' *Unemployment Unit Bulletin*, November 1983

31. Brenner, H — 'The Effects of the Economy on Criminal Behaviour and the Administration of Criminal Justice in the United States, Canada, England, Wales and Scotland' in *Economic Crises and Crime*, Rome: UNSDRI 1976

32. Bradshaw, J — 'A Taxonomy of Social Need', in G McLachland (ed) *Problems and Progress in Medical Care*, Oxford University Press, 1972

CHAPTER TWO

1. Buckle, J R — 'Work and Housing of Impaired Persons 'in Great Britain', Part Two of *Handicapped and Impaired in Great Britain*, HMSO, 1971
2. 'Characteristics of the Unemployed: Sample Survey June 1976', *Department of Employment Gazette*, June 1977
3. Daniel, W W — *A National Survey of the Unemployed*, PEP, 1974
4. Manpower Services Commission — *Review of Services for the Unemployed*, MSC, March 1981
5. White, M — *Long Term Unemployment and Labour Markets*, PSI, 1984
6. Walker, A — *Unqualified and Underemployed* Handicapped Young People and the Labour Market, National Children's Bureau, 1982
7. Townsend, P — 'The Government Must Do Its Sums Better', *The Disability Rights Handbook*, 1984
8. Walker, A — 'Disability', *New Society*, 22/29, December 1984
9. HMSO — *Better Services for the Mentally Handicapped* Cmnd 4683, June 1971
10. Massie, B — 'International Year of Disabled People: Was it Worth It?' in *Year Book of Social Policy in Britain*, 1982, Routledge and Kegan Paul, 1983
11. Kettle, M — 'Works Wonders', *The Guardian*, 14/11/84

CHAPTER THREE

1. Stein, M, Carey, K and Taylor, P — Leaving Care Project, Centre for Social Work and Applied Social Studies, University of Leeds. Research still in Progress.
2. Burgess, C — *In Care and Into Work*, Tavistock, 1981
3. The Tavistock Institute of Human Relations — 'Transitions from Care' research currently in progress
4. Department of Health and Social Security — *Child Care Act 1980: Children in Care in England and Wales, March 1982*, DHSS, 1984
5. DHSS — Op cit, 1984
6. Loughran, F — Unpublished research conducted at the Department of Social Administration, University of Bristol

7. Strathclyde Regional Council — 'Costs and Impact of Unemployment'. Report by the Chief Executive to the Policy and Resources Committee, May 1981

8. Porter, R — *Teenagers Leaving Care*, University of East Anglia, 1984

9. Gulbenkian Foundation — *Broadcasting and Youth*, Gulkenkian Foundation, 1979

10. Total numbers of children in care for each authority obtained from *Personal Social Services Statistics, 1984-85 Estimates*, Chartered Institute of Public Finance and Accountancy, July 1984

CHAPTER FOUR

1. Jahoda, M — *Marienthal: The Sociography of an Unemployed Community*, Tavistock Publications, 1933 (re-issued 1972)

2. Fagin, L and Little, M — *The Forsaken Families*, Chapter Five Pelican, 1984

3. Colledge, M and Bartholomew, R — *A Study of the Long-Term Unemployed*, MSC, 1980.

4. Brenner, M H — 'Mortality and the National Economy. 'A Review of the Experience of England and Wales 1936-1976', *The Lancet*, 15 September 1979

5. Moser K A, Fox A J and Jones D R — 'Unemployment and Mortality', *The Lancet*, 8 December 1984

6. Warr P — 'A Study of Psychological Well-Being', *British Journal of Psychology*, Part One, 1978

7. Daniel W W — *A National Survey of the Unemployed*, PEP, 1974

8. Fagin L, & Little M — Op cit, 1984

9. Office of Population Census and Surveys — *OPCS Monitor DH4/81/4*, 6 October 1981

10. Moser, Fox and Jones — Op cit

11. Platt S — 'Unemployment and Para-Suicide in Edinburgh, 1962-1982', *Unemployment Unit Bulletin, No 10*, 1983

12. Fryer D and Warr P — 'Unemployment and Cognitive Difficulties', *British Journal of Clinical Psychology*, Volume 23, Part One, February 1984

13. Francis L J — *Youth and Unemployment*, Costello, 1984

14. Breakwell G et al — 'Attitudes Towards the Unemployed: Effects of Threatened Identity', *British Journal of Social Psychology*,Volume 23, Part One, February 1984

15. House of Commons — *Community Care*: Second Report from the Social Services Committee, HMSO, 1985

16. Birch A — 'What Chance Have We Got?', Manchester Mind, 1983

17. Birch A — Op cit

18. Hayes J and Nutman P — *Understanding the Unemployed*, Tavistock Publications, 1981

19. Storr A — 'Out of Mind', *Sunday Times*, 6 January 1985

CHAPTER FIVE

1. Harris M — 'How Unemployment Affects People', *New Society*, 14 January 1984

2. Department of Employment — *Family Expenditure Survey 1983*, HMSO, 1983

3. Bradshaw J, Cooke K, and Godfrey, C — 'The Impact of Unemployment on Living Standards of Families' from the *Journal of Social Policy* October 1983

4. Daniel, WW — *A National Survey of the Unemployed*, PEP, 1974

5. Report of a Joint Working Party of Directors of Social Services and the Welsh Office — 'The Implications of Rising Unemployment for Personal Social Services in Wales', March 1981

6. City of Newcastle upon Tyne — 'High Unemployment in the Inner City; the Impact on Local Government and the Community', 1982

7. Strathclyde Regional Council — 'Cost and Impact of Unemployment'. Report by the Chief Executive to the Policy and Resources Committee, May 1981

8. Sheffield City Council — 'Indicators of Need', Internal Document, 24 August 1981

9. West Midlands Citizens Advice Bureau — 'Debt in the Recession', Report of the Money Advice Development Project, January 1983

CHAPTER SIX

1. Brenner H — 'Effects of the Economy on Criminal Behaviour in the Administration of Criminal Justice in the US, Canada, England and Wales and Scotland', in *Economic Crisis and Crime*, UNSDRI, Rome, 1976

2. Tarling R — 'Unemployment and Crime', *Home Office Research Bulletin, No 14*

3. Carr Hill R A and Stern N H — *Crime, the Police and Criminal Statistics*, Academic Press, 1979

4. Gladstone D — 'Crime and the Crystal Ball', *Home Office Research Bulletin*, No 7, 1979

5. Phillips L, Votey H L and Maxwell D — 'Crime, Youth and the Labour Market', *Journal of Political Economy*, 80, 1972

6. McLintock F H — 'Unemployment and Criminality', in *Economic Crisis and Crime*, Op cit, UNSDRI, 1976

7. Rainer Foundation — Lewisham study, 'Analysis of Court Proceedings, August — May 1983', unpublished

8. National Association for the Care and Resettlement of Offenders — Analysis of Records for Trainees, Second Quarter, 1983. NACRO YTS Schemes, unpublished

9. Lewis J — 'Unemployment and Offenders: The Probation Service Response', M.SC, Dissertation, LSE, unpublished.

10. Box J and Hale L — 'Economic Crisis and the Rising Prisoner Population in England and Wales', in *Crime and Social Justice*, No 17, July 1982

11. Department of Health and Social Security — 'Offending by Young People: A Survey of Recent Trends', DHSS, p 41, paragraph 35

12. Home Office — 'Cautioning by the Police: A Consultative Document', Home Office, 1984 (12)

13. House of Lords — NACRO's Submission to the House of Lords Select Committee on Unemployment, HMSO, 1982

14. Morris P — 'A Good Heart is not Enough', *Community Care*, 9 February 1984

15. IT Evaluation Project directed by Professor A E Bottoms, Institute of Criminology, Cambridge

16. National Association for the Care and Resettlement of Offenders — 'CAYO', 'Community Alternatives for Young Offenders' Final Report, NACRO, 1982

17. 'Persons Found Guilty at Magistrates Courts of Indictable Offences by Petty Sessional Division and Sentence'. Statistics supplied by the Home Office

18. London Borough of Lambeth — Lambeth Intermediate Treatment Directory

CHAPTER SEVEN

1. Nash, M — 'The Importance of Unemployment in the Referrals to a Social Services Team'. Reception Team Peterborough Division, December 1981 – January 1982,

unpublished.

2. Strathclyde Regional Council — Talbot Initiative Group, Report by the Director of Social Work, 1983

CHAPTER EIGHT

1. See Chapter 2
2. See Chapter 3
3. See Chapter 4
4. See Appendix D
5. See Chapter 6
6. See Chapter 5
7. See Chapter 7
8. See Chapter 3, paragraph 37-46
9. See Chapter 3, ibid
10. See Chapter 3, paragraph 11-23
11. Centre for Environmental Studies — *The Outer Estates*, CES, 1984
12. Department of Health and Social Security — Report on Local Authority Expenditure for the years 1983-84 to 1986-87 by the Expenditure Group for the Personal Social Services, Port Health and Sheltered Employment, July 1984
13. See Chapter 5
14. Association of Directors of Social Services — 'Unemployment and Care Services', ADSS Parliamentary Committee Briefing Note, 12 November 1984

APPENDIX C

1. Department of the Environment, Inner Cities Directorate — *Urban Deprivation*, DOE Information Note No 2, 1983

APPENDIX D

1. Creighton, S J — Trends in Child Abuse, NSPCC, 1984
2. Burghes, L — 'Children in Poverty', *Concern* No 50, Spring 1984